What can this book

- If you are stuck or blocked from moving forward, you may find some strategies that could help.

- If you are feeling inadequate or not worthy for any reason this could help you discover that you are already more than enough.

- If you think that the universe has singled you out for a particular challenge, I hope this book will help you understand that you are not alone.

In this book, I have opened up to you in a way I have never done before, to share my thoughts and experiences to help you to be equally honest with yourself. And I know how easy we all are to convince ourselves of anything!

What people are saying about Moses

Bulgarian athlete Ivet Goranova, was coached by Moses to Gold Medal success in the Tokyo Olympic Games 2021. Moses worked with her on a daily basis in the run-up to the tournament to get her thinking like a champion and she won Bulgaria's first Olympic Gold Medal in 13 years.

Says Ivet "I am very happy to have met Moses at the perfect time. I trusted him from the beginning. For me, he has been a magician by turning my thoughts into realities!

Moses is a man of faith and victories. He has improved my personal life and helped me achieve my biggest dreams.

He believes that, in order to get uncommon results you must be willing to do uncommon things. He constantly told me, 'if not you, who else?'

Moses told me that I was an Olympic champion long before I had even done it. Since we've been working together, I feel like whatever I set my sights on will become a reality."

Ivet Goranova - Olympic Gold Medallist

2020 Summer Olympic Games.

Andy Harrington

Firstly, a massive congratulations to Moses Nalocca for this amazing masterpiece.

As founder of the Professional Speakers Academy, my passion is teaching talented business owners how to craft a presentation that impacts, inspires and makes income through the acquisition of new clients.

It is rare to find a coach with a powerful skill set and a proven success record of helping people to win whether that be winning in life, business or an Olympic medal.

When I first met Moses, immediately recognized a coach with the ability to inspire and motivate others in a lasting way.

He is a natural communicator on stage and full of energy.

Few people have the talent and confidence to address an arena of 5,000 people, but Moses can!

He really is a master of his craft, and I'm so thrilled and delighted that he's also chosen to be an ambassador supporting our Professional Speakers Academy members.

I congratulate Moses and I know he will be making an ever-greater impact
around the world in the years ahead.

Maybe you picked up this book in a bookstore or library? Or perhaps you bought it on Amazon or received it as a gift? However, you came to have hold of this book, you have one of life's little gems.

I wish you all health, wealth, and happiness.
Andy Harrington - Sunday Times
Best Selling.
Author of Passion Into Profit.
Presentation-Profits.com

Moses "I have asked Andy to give you a gift to add value to you.Just click on the link.

Rich Waterman

"I have had the pleasure of coaching Moses for quite a few years. I first met him when he attended a workshop I was running. Two things immediately struck me at that first meeting - his energy and his presence. He is a phenomenal human being. He has an incredible appetite to grow, so that he can serve others even more.

It is an absolute privilege to work with this man. He has the biggest heart and I would recommend that anyone should interact with either his speaking or coaching. Ideally both!" -

Rich Waterman

"I asked Rich to share something with you that
could add massive value to you.
He has gift for you access to his online tool box.
Just click on the link below

https://bit.ly/richtoolbox

It doesn't matter where you
are in life right now,
keep on moving.
Take one step at a time.
God gave us feet to move,
he didn't give us roots
to stay at one place.
You get true fulfillment only
when there's progress.

Moses

Martin Sharp

Be more to give more! What a fabulous value to live by, and live by it Moses does, in his book More! Moses takes you through several stories from his life of how his consistent drive to become more has helped to serve thousands of people, including working with those in the upper echelons of their fields, such as helping Olympians take home the gold medal,

Business owners develop 10-100x growth in their ventures and C-Level executives go all in taking their firms to greater success in the cut-throat corporate world.

As a busy entrepreneur, I have been blessed to work with Moses, helping him go from a post-Covid 87kg, feeling lethargic, with brain fog and lacking the body that he once had, to reliving whom he is, regaining his amazing confidence and energy, looking fabulously congruent in his crusade to awaken others to the power they have to live, lead and love an even better life. Because sometimes you need to put yourself first to have an even greater positive impact in the world, to be selfish in order to be selfless.

If you believe that you want to have a positive effect in the lives of others, then I recommend that you read More! for a practical example of what it takes and where it can take you.

MARTIN SHARP
Multi-Award Winning International Consultant, Coach, Speaker and Author

Moses "I have asked Martin to give you a gift to add value to your journey. This link will introduce you to "The Power of AND" introducing a life of combination that shared at TEDx talk is the basis for significant personal and social change along with business acceleration!
www.sharpfitforlife.com

ABOUT MOSES NALOCCA

His entrepreneurial spirit led Moses to open his first business when he was only 23 years old. Since then, Moses has mastered the skill of High-Performance Coaching and has been helping his clients to level up in life and businesses by removing self-sabotaging beliefs and helping them solve burning problems.

In 2019 he went to Bulgaria to represent and develop the market for Tony Robbins and Success Resources. Back in the days, Moses broke all sales records for Success Resources as a Business Mastery leading consultant using High-Performance Coaching Skills. Now, Moses is on a mission to train 1000 new coaches and trainers by 2025 through his Upper Echelon Coaching Academy.

He has worked closely with some of the most admired people in business and self-actualization, such as Robert Kiyosaki, Gary Vaynerchuk, and Tony Robbins, to name a few.

He has trained the leaders of Philip Morris International, TechoArena, Transpress, iBrokers, FitLine, Oriflame, Entegra, BulMed Consulting, Happy Bar and Grill, and UXP, as well as the Gold Olympic Medalist in Karate 2020 – Ivet Goranova and many more.

Ask for MORE,
and be ready to get it

Most people never experience deep fulfillment, true happiness or solid success. But why is that?

Are they unlucky? Is fate unfair to them? Is it just not meant to be? Well, the answer is actually pretty simple – they have no idea that they can take control over their life. That's why they live within their own mental cage, sabotage themselves with limiting beliefs, and obey the negative emotions.

Fortunately, a slight shift in perspectives can change the whole picture. Using coaching and NLP techniques as a foundation, Moses Nalocca helps people all over the world to see reality from a different angle and turn the mess into a miracle. He can support you in creating the life you're yearning for. Take your relationships, business, health, and personal growth to the next level. Start your journey now.

The companion volume to this book is the Moses Nalocca Gratitude Journal. Go to www.mosesnalocca.com/book/journal

Dedication

I dedicate this book to...

My Mom who believed in me
and has always been there
for me through all my ups
and downs in life.

My Gift to You

I am really grateful that you have chosen to join me on my own journey of discovery and are allowing me to share the same insights that I had when presented with challenging circumstances, or at important moments of decision. Each fork in the road that we choose to take, means that we have also chosen no to go in the alternative direction, so choice determines where we end up and who we become.

When we embark on a journey we need to pack the things we will need to take with us. On this journey one of the most important things you will need is an attitude of gratitude and the ability to quietly meditate. So, my gift to you, as you set off, is one of the best practical tools I know, to help you with this.

I am inviting you to listen to a guided meditation, where I will take you through Three Steps of Gratitude. I know for sure that you have wealth inside of you, you've got emotional wealth, you've got physical wealth, you've got memories wealth, so you are already wealthy. This tool I am gifting you will help you to understand this on an even deeper level.

Just scan to get your free gift. Enjoy!

Acknowledgements

I would like to acknowledge my mother for being that pillar of our family and a rock for me. You have always taught me never to settle for mediocrity.

To my brother and his family for always making me feel loved and special.

To my clients, for having trusted me with their minds, their hearts and their lives. For their trust in my belief in them, well before they had belief in themselves.

To Totka Spasova who believed in me long before I had the courage to do so myself. Without her belief, love, and support, I would not be where I am now.

A special acknowledgment to all my mentors and coaches, present and past, visible and invisible. Thanks for seeding greatness in me.

Special acknowledgment to my long term best friend Danilo Fazzi Amici. A true friend is someone who consciously decides to stay by your side even though they are aware of your weaknesses. Thanks for being a great supporter, ready even to drive 7000 km just to pick me up during lockdown.

Last but not least thanks to God Who trusts me to help and impact millions of people.

Thank you!

I tell my athletes,
your battle,
your competition
is not against anybody
else and certainly
not against your opponent.
Your biggest battle
is with yourself.

Moses

Moses Nalocca

MORE

BECOME MORE - GIVE MORE

Published by
AUTHORITIZE
14, Croydon Road, Beddington,
Croydon, Surrey, CR0 4PA
+44 (0) 208 688 2598
www.authoritize.co.uk

MORE by Moses Nalocca

ISBN 978-1-913623-82-1

Editor - Christopher Day

Cover Design Ian Henderson 2-h.co.uk

Table of Contents

Chapter One
Where are you heading?

I believe that life is a wonderful gift.
We have all been showered with gifts, skills, and insights. We have been surrounded by people, places, and possibilities.

So why is it that, right now, we are not where we so rightly deserve to be?

Why is it that we have yet to achieve our goals?
Is life getting in our way, or are we getting in the way of our life?

Well?

Have you ever had the frustration of taking one big step forward, only to find that soon afterward, you have lost ground and have taken fifteen steps backward? Why was that?

Have you ever felt trapped in your life, like being trapped in a maze with no obvious exit? And no Google maps!

All of us are looking for answers to solve the puzzle that life has given to us.

So where are you now with your life right now?

Maybe you have been disappointed by somebody you truly believed in or loved. (It happens) which could mean you may be afraid to open up and trust again.

Perhaps you may have faced an unexpected setback that wasn't caused by you and you are looking for answers or solutions. Does this mean you may have not given up on your blaming list, blaming your family, employer, economy and also the weather?

Potentially, the big dream you had for your life seems to be being snatched away from you and you are overwhelmed with doubts and uncertainty. Has this made you fearful for the future?

Possibly, as you look ahead on your chosen journey, do you feel that you are alone? Do you no longer feel understood or supported?

Ask any successful person how was he able to conquer the peaks that he is proudly standing on today, and he will tell you that he did not do it alone.

Behind the backs of some of the best athletes, business managers, artists and politicians in the world, there are some exceptional mentors standing in order to guide them and to help them express their best.

They are surrounded by people who believe in them. You can find your "support" in the face of the coaching expert Moses Nalocca and other brave entrepreneurs who understand your purposes and are ready to help you achieving them.

You can be the same

So where do you see yourself heading:

What possibilities are waiting further down the road?

What reward is waiting for you just over the horizon?

Imagine the time when you have achieved your goals and are looking back on a job well done, which means deleting something from your wish list and looking forward for the next big step

Envisage your life surrounded by the people you love, giving you support and encouragement. Which means love is at the centre of your life, now you are not alone and life has become an amazing adventure.

Picture the time when you have achieved the financial, health, emotional, and spiritual success you had planned for. Picture having the freedom to choose, what to do, how to do it and with who to do it.

Visualize yourself proud of the person you have become, which means finally you can be satisfied with the person you see in the mirror and now you can give and contribute to others.

Doesn't that feel good?

Why are you reading this book <u>now?</u>

Have you taken the decision that now is the time to change?

Are you fed up with being who you are or where you are?

Have you decided that there could be more in your life?

If so, I can help you as a coach, by stepping back and giving you a fresh perspective to look at your big picture. We are all too close to our problems. We are also too close to see the true value of the many gifts we have been given, and to fully understand the reason we have been created.

Life is now. You can't change the past and neither can you control what will happen tomorrow. The only time you can live is now, in the present.
NOW is the moment. Now is the time you have got to live.

Let me help you on that journey by first helping you understand that there is no magic pill, no clever life hack, and no shortcut. Sometimes it can take ten years to become an overnight success!

I have always been sceptical of so-called gurus promising overnight success. I prefer to remain grounded and live in the real world.

We all started our journeys a long time ago. We have been making regular payments into our "Bank of Knowledge" so by now we should all have a healthy credit balance. Now is the time to make a withdrawal of the knowledge you have accumulated, and put it to good use. Use it or lose it! You don't want to end up with a dormant account! I want you to use your knowledge to unlock new possibilities so you can be MORE than you are now. The seeds are already inside you.

Through this book, I will share with you my philosophy, my attitude, and what has helped me personally, to navigate to where I am now which, by the way, is not yet where I want to be. It's a journey!

As you will read in the following chapters, my own life has been one long quest to overcome adversity and find my true path. On that journey I found myself taking the wrong path only too often, falling down, yes, but picking myself up and moving forward.

I do hope that my journey will help to give you some "Ah-ha" moments to inspire you to achieve your own greatness.

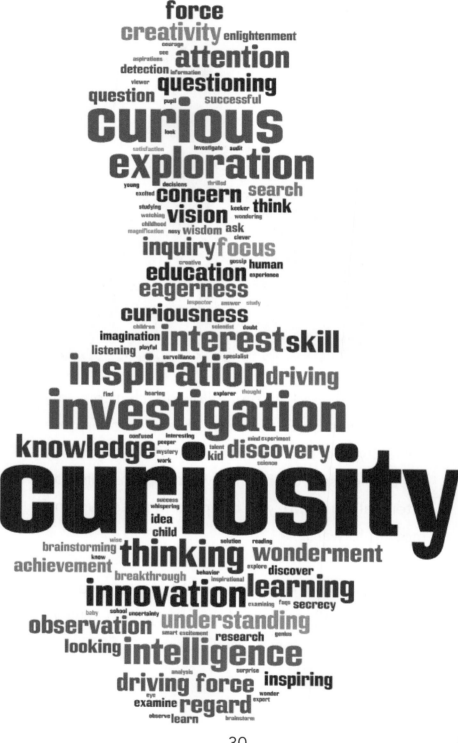

Chapter Two
Curiosity

From an early age, I have been curious. Curious about things, curious about people. What makes them tick? Why do some people succeed, and some people don't? Why are some people open and positive and others negative? I have always wondered.

When somebody achieves great success, I am not envious, quite the reverse. I celebrate success, but I am also curious about it. I am interested in how they achieved it. What they did. My question is always, can I do the same? Can I repeat what they did? What is the formula? What is the recipe? Can I do it better? Can I add more value? What can I learn? I have grown up looking at things and people in a different way.

I have always been passionate about being a trailblazer and not only doing things that have not been done before, but helping my clients to do the same.

As a kid, I remember watching Nelson Mandela receive the Nobel Peace Prize. Bill Clinton, Barack

IT'S IN YOUR HANDS TO MAKE A BETTER WORLD FOR ALL WHO LIVE IN IT

-NELSON MANDELA-

Obama. All of them are great inspirational leaders who I grew up admiring.

All of them were great orators and received global recognition.

We all need role models to look up to.

All of these giants had to start from somewhere. All of them, and all of us, have to take our journey through life one step at a time, and one mistake at a time.

My journey was influenced by other greats. Zig Ziglar, Les Brown, Jim Rohn – who spent 25 years broke until someone helped him to change his mindset.

Finally, the great Tony Robbins has had a massive influence on my life. We never need to look far for people to guide us – but we do need to look.

I believe that everyone needs a coach or mentor who can step back and see more than we can. Someone who has been down the road ahead, and has come back down to guide us along the path.

In my story, I will be sharing with you those pivotal moments that have brought me to today and hopefully will stop you from making the many mistakes that I did.

I have been privileged to be helped by many amazing people. I have found that whenever I had a need, the Universe always brought the right person to me to help with it.

I will be eternally grateful to my coach Rich Waterman who helped me become more than I thought I could.

I must also thank Andy Harrington, the founder of the Professional Speakers Academy, the best peer group you could have.

I related to Andy because we had much in common. We both had a similar life journey. His parents divorced when he was 13. He had a massive breakup and got divorced. This turned out to be a turning point for him, as it was a turning point for me.

Andy had an incredible loss in his family. Like me, he lost his son and I lost my little brother. We also had in common an appreciation for Tony Robbins.

The Professional Speakers Academy is an amazing community of speakers that are constantly always supporting each other to grow, to evolve, and to improve. By applying the techniques that I learned there, my speaking career moved up to another level until I got to a point where I was speaking in front of 5,000 people in an arena.

I thought it was amazing that the young boy who was so shy that he hid behind the sound desk, and the waiter who was running away from his call, could end up on such a large stage.

Yet there is more. I was privileged to join Andy Harrington's personal team as a coach, to support the delegates in the next steps in their speaking career. And also, as a coach, to support and help train the sales team by showing them how to effectively communicate.

I spent eight months doing this and helping to grow the Academy to a high level.

I found myself being recognized by the Academy by being presented with the award of Sales Person of the Year.

Then I was further recognized for my achievements by personally generating over one million pounds in sales and impacting thousands of people along the way. Andy Harrington presented me with the Seven Figure Award.

Now, it's not about the money or the numbers achieved but in a world where numbers count, money is just a reflection of how many people I have helped. It's about the people that I have reached. It's about the people that have made a change, or a transformation and moved foward to where they wanted to be. That's what it's all about.

**Moses receives the Seven Figure Award
from Andy Harrington**

So, what is your call? What is your mission? If you don't know where you are going, you may well end up somewhere else!

How do you find your mission? If you don't know, you need to start your quest to find out. What do you need to do?

Firstly, be the best version of yourself that you can be.

Second, listen to the Universe for clues. If you cut out the noise, you will hear.

Thirdly, by doing 300% on what you're doing right now, no matter how menial it is.

I did my 300% while I was working as a bartender and as a waiter. When I was working in the sales team I did my 300% there as well. Wherever I have been I've done my 300% starting from the bottom, to end up on the top. For example, when I was 16, I started as the boy who was tidying up the beach in my city on the seaside. After less than 2 years I was managing a team of waiters planning their shifts and taking care of the most important thing: the reservations.

I wanted to be ready for when the universe looks at me and asks, "Are you ready for the next level? If so, here you go!"

I needed to be ready and equipped for my next opportunity.

Let me be honest with you, I haven't even scratched the surface. There are more layers down there and more levels upward. I have only just begun. I know definitely, that there is MORE waiting for me ahead.

It's time for you
to see yourself
as a truly
amazing being,
to rise above
your limitations.
You need
to explore
your potential.

Moses Nalocca

Chapter Three

We all have to start somewhere

I very nearly didn't make it into this world. I was born in Uganda in the final days of Idi Amin's regime. Actually Idi Amin was removed in 1979, then Uganda went into a period called The Ugandan Bush War, also known as the Luwero War, the Ugandan Civil War or the Resistance War, it was a civil war fought in Uganda by the official Ugandan government and its armed wing, the Uganda National Liberation Army (UNLA), against a number of rebel groups, most importantly the National Resistance Army (NRA), from 1980 to 1986. I was born in 1984. It was a brutal time and the soldiers were also persecuting Christians.

Later I was told that, at one point, soldiers came to our house and beat up both my father and mother, who was pregnant with me. Scared that she might lose me, they went to the hospital to be checked out. Fortunately, we were both OK.

I must have been born with a purpose, because I couldn't wait to come into the world and get started. I was born nearly two and a half months early. I was tiny. I mean TINY! I spend my first days and weeks in an incubator fighting for life but fight I did.

Life is such a precious gift and I couldn't wait to live it. We are born with a purpose. Everyone of us! It is our quest to find out what it is. Nobody is a mistake.

I was very close to my Mom and I will never forget the time I saw her crying uncontrollably. It was in July, which ever since then has been a painful time. I had a brother, Joshua. He was four or five and was leaving Kindergarten to get the bus home. He wasn't properly helped to cross the road and was hit by a car.

At that same moment, my Mom was coming out of the hospital at the end of her shift and she passed the ambulance bringing in her son. She arrived home to find Joshua not there. At the time there are no cell phones, and it was really difficult to find out where he was. Sadly, he passed away before she could find him.

My dad was away working in Paris at the time and it took him a couple of days to get back, I remember him being totally devastated. I remember him getting out of the yellow car and three people from the church supporting him as he couldn't walk. That's the only time I saw him crying, vulnerable and lost. As a small kid of 5 or 6 years, my dad was a giant, tall and strong and it was strange to see him crying and being held by others.

Looking back, I never really understood my Dad. Frankly, he never gave me the chance to do so. He was a quiet man but could have a fiery temper. One happy memory of him was when my smallest brother was born, John Mark. I remember going with him to buy flowers and chocolates for my mum in the hospital. It was a happy memory with my Dad as we went to see my new tiny brother.

Sadly, I have few memories like this. My dad was emotionally and physically "absent" for much of my life. However, there was one point when he was very much there.

I have to say that my mum has always been able to forgive. She even forgave the driver who killed her son. I know that she also forgave my dad for not being there when she needed him the most.

For years I used to blame my dad. Then I would blame my mum. But now, as a coach, I know that you can't point the finger of blame at anyone. When you point at someone, there are always three fingers pointing back at you.

Nobody has the right to apportion blame. Nobody can know the pain that another person is going through. Nobody knows all of the facts. Nobody has the right to judge anyone else.

I think one of the things that drew me towards becoming a coach was my need to understand what drives people and how they heal themselves. My upbringing has been very helpful on this journey.

Following the death of my brother Joshua, we were fractured as a family and it was a very raw time for me. At school, when there was a poem or any mention of death there was an anchoring of pain. I used to break down and cry. I couldn't help it.

The culture in Uganda is to celebrate a life rather than mourn a death. There is music, food, and dancing. My last memory of Joshua was in his coffin. He is sleeping, they kept telling me.

"When will he wake up so we can play?" I asked. "No, he is sleeping" was all they would say.

I didn't quite understand what was going on, all family was there around this small white coffin and I remember the moment they had to close it, they sent me out with my other cousins and then we travelled to my father's village. Both my mum and I had to put off our grieving till much later. I found it very difficult. From that moment I was afraid of dying. When the subject of death came up, I was blocked. I would be paralyzed. I would think of Joshua and break down. I would say "Why Joshua? Why? Why? Why?" time and time again. I was caught in the headlights. I needed to find a way to heal.

It wasn't that I was just paralyzed, I also realized that at that time I was running away from my calling, from my purpose. I was running away from my life. I was afraid of leaving. I was afraid of dying. I was afraid of tomorrow. I was stuck.

So what was my calling? I wasn't sure. I knew that I didn't want to be a Pastor like my mother, but I did know that I wanted to work with people and to impact them in some way. That would be a worthwhile purpose. The shifting point for me, and when I managed to heal myself, was when I realized that becoming an author, a coach, and a speaker I can leave a bit of me inside everyone I help on their journeys. If I can do that I will never die. I will live on in them. That realization gave me back my purpose and helped me to move on.

In September 1990, my dad's work required him to move to Italy and naturally, we all had to follow. I was about to experience a massive cultural change in my life. The family is about to move from Uganda to Italy. Not just a different culture but a different language. I didn't know any Italian! It wasn't easy for me and I am sure it was even more difficult for my parents. We were all coming from an Equatorial hot country to Autumn in Europe and I experienced snow for the first time. I went from Summer T-shirts and shorts to winter gloves, a hat, and a thick coat. The cold was a real shock.

In Uganda, I had gone through primary school and knew how to read and write the alphabet in English. Now, at six years, all I had to do was to apply these basic skills to Italian. Everyone in the class was also learning to read and write so we were all learning together. My Mum encouraged me in my studies and taught me to always aim high in all my exams. She was a very positive influence on me and always promoted Bible principles. This stood me in good stead throughout my education. When I went to Junior school I realized that I wasn't as "cool" as the other boys, I didn't have fancy jeans and hoodies, at that time they were so popular the "Energie" Brand or I didn't have the latest Nike shoes: the Air Zoom or the new Air max.

My father used to say: "they are too expensive, we cannot afford them" So he would provide us

FLASHBACK TO '95.

PART 3: NIKE AIR MAX UPTEMPO

with cheap shoes that most of the time would break or tear after a couple of months. This scarcity mentality of my dad had serious consequences on my financial journey.

At that time I was angry with my parents, I was constantly wondering:

"Why?"
Why can't I have those shoes?
Why can't I have that Hoodie?
Why can't I be as cool as the football captain of our local team, as my football mates"
I developed an inferiority complex.
That was the moment I realized:
I was different,
I was Black,
I wasn't understood,

I wasn't popular.
Can You relate to me?
I started to be more conscious of where I was, and

with who. I started to hide as much as possible so people would not notice that I didn't have a cool jacket or tracksuit.

When I went to junior school I really started to feel uncomfortable. After football training sessions, my schoolmates would go to the bar and have ice cream or a Coke and then play table tennis or video games. My parents were not providing pocket money for me to spend in bars, and they expected me to get back home and focus on my books.

I was constantly looking for ways of avoiding the spotlight and I developed great skills in listening, suddenly I became the best friend of the girls.

Girls were accepting me as I was, without any comparisons, or judging. Quickly in the school, the word spread as "Moses the boy who talks and understands girls". Every girl wanted to talk to me, they were feeling safe, heard, and noticed, because I wasn't judging them. Now I realize where my skills as a coach started to develop. Girls just needed somebody ready and available just to listen and to be honest. Boys felt uncomfortable talking to girls. For many boys, external appearance, cool clothes, and expensive shoes were everything. They lacked the courage to talk to girls.

So girls started to ask me for advice on how to deal with boys, school or issues with parents and family.

Surprisingly also, boys now started to come to me as well, and ask me things. I remember a girl that I really liked came to me for advice. I didn't dare to tell her of my feelings. She started to talk about the most handsome boy in the school. I found myself putting aside the feelings I had for her then and helped her to get together. She never knew how I felt for her.

I was just the boy providing help and solutions. I was too busy helping others that I didn't have time to find a girlfriend of my own.

On one hand, I was happy that my level of significance had skyrocketed. Suddenly, I was the wise guy to go to talk to, where you could feel understood and not judged, where you could feel safe.

I vividly remember the mother of one of my best friends comparing my maturity with the one of a forty-year-old responsible man.

So whatever age you are, whether you are a teenager (and already know it all) or if you are at the opposite end of the age range, it is never too late to achieve your dreams and find your true purpose.

For me, a great gift was that of curiosity. Wanting to find out more about everything around me. Wanting to know how somebody achieved something. Wanting to find out how everything works. How can I get out of a situation? How can I make a difference? How can I get MORE?

Even when I watch a documentary or a movie about a person, I don't rely on what is on screen, I get my phone out and research the full story to find out what has been missed out.

I am just curious about people, life and everything. And always will be.

Habits have an effect
on your identity.
They are predictors
of success
or the lack of it.

Moses Nalocca

Chapter Four

The Power of Dreams

In my formative years, I was never accepted by my peer group because my focus was on different things to them. They were looking at football as being their way to escape the life they had. I wasn't obsessed with it. At a very young age, after football training, they would go to the bar and play table tennis. For me, I just wanted to get back home, do my study and finish my homework.

At school, there was one teacher who scared me. This is the maths teacher in junior school 1995-1996 and 1996-1997. A short man with a moustache, I used to describe him as Lenin.

-"Nalocca, come to the blackboard and solve this equation"
-"Yes professor"

As I walk to the blackboard I'm dreadfully scared of making a mistake. I solve the equation and put

back the white chalk and he looks at me, erases the equation without telling me if it was correct and writes a new one –"this time explain the steps and the process to get to the answer."

"Yes sir" I start to solve the equation then I speak with a low voice.

-"raise your voice"

-"mhh…X..equals to…"

-"louder…!!!!"

-"…X…equals to"

-"louder, I can't hear you!" I was terrorized

-"X…X..e..equ..equals…" at this point I'm stuttering while he is screaming at me to speak out louder. It was embarrassing. I can feel the eyes of my classmates, I feel so small and insignificant.

Since then when I'm under pressure I stutter. Not a helpful quality for my later life on stage. Many years later I'm grateful for that horrible experience, the year later I was in another school, another city, another teacher and I'm getting the best grades in maths.

After my original negative experience with maths, I was doing extra exercises, other equations, getting better and faster.

All of us have two main fears. One is the fear of not being good enough, the other is the fear of not being loved or being rejected. I had these same two fears with my team mates, in the local football team. I wanted to be loved, accepted, and wanted by them and I didn't want to feel out of place. It is only natural. But let me ask you.

Why should you fit in, when you have been created to stand out?

Dr. Seuss

Looking back, I can see that when I first started hanging around with my football team mates and accepting their behaviours and attitudes, was the time when my own marks at school started dropping, And I really mean dropping!

It took me a while to realize what was happening and to put cause and effect together. In the back of my mind, I had some big dreams. I wanted to be a great ambassador or a great politician. I wanted to impact the world and be educated like them. With this group around me, this was never going to be the outcome. So I made a decision.

I dropped the team and all of the people in it, who had no ambition or direction, and chose to refocus on my academic studies.

I had tried to please my friends and to be accepted, I wanted to be a part of their world, their community, but it wasn't working. It did not take long to turn things around and for my grades to improve. I finished junior school with an

excellent mark.   But did I learn the lesson? Probably not!

Books and music became my hiding place, this is where I could be myself with no mask or no intention to prove anything to anybody.

When I was with my books and music, and keyboard I was happy, smiling, and excited.

I first started public speaking at the age of 14. It was 1997 and at that time I was living in Rome. My Mom was attending a Bible school. We all travelled to see the great preachers when they spoke at conferences locally to us, in front of thousands of people. I was amazed at how they spoke with so much eloquence and fluidity and inspired the audience.

At that time, I was a real introvert. I enjoyed being with myself and being in silence. I didn't like being in the spotlight. A complete contrast to who I have become today is when I am the one speaking on stage talking to thousands of people around the world. Now it is me being interviewed in newspapers, appearing on television, and coaching Olympic athletes.

Back then, whilst my Mom attending events, I would be hiding at the back of the room on the sound desk just listening and looking at these amazing speakers, while I was completely invisible to everyone.

I was fascinated by how somebody could use their words and their enthusiasm to connect with an audience and inspire them.

Always, when they were on stage, they would be wearing a suit so that inspired me to dress the same and to be smart. That has stayed with me ever since.

In 1998 Mom was organizing services and activities for Christmas in our local church. She asked me to get involved and to help her with looking after the children. So, it was then that I found myself speaking on stage in front of a hundred people. I found that I wasn't afraid and could speak confidently on stage. So that is where it all started. They would also encourage me to sing, which I enjoyed, so music also became an important aspect of my world.

Working with the Youth Group every Sunday I felt in my element. No matter what would happen during the week, I would always look forward to Sunday morning and working with them. I was able to develop my speaking and storytelling skills. It was a special time. I wasn't talking about spiritual matters but rather things to inspire and motivate them.

I found myself listening to their problems and their difficulties at school and instinctively tried to give them advice. When you are a teenager, every problem with school, a relationship, or with a family member, feels like the end of the world simply because you don't have the strategies to deal with them. Having been through the same things myself, I did have some experience to draw from. I would work with some of them individually to help them through a crisis and to this day I still have letters from some of them thanking me for encouraging them. I suppose this was the start of, what became, my coaching career.

At High School, I smashed it for the first few years until, once again, I got distracted again by the wrong peer group. I am only human! I stopped focusing on my academic life. The need for me to be wanted and accepted was still strong so I put myself forward for election to the Student Council and I also got involved in politics. This took me in all sorts of directions and activities. Everybody knew me. I was involved with everything, except my studies.

My teachers encouraged me to stand for school president. They felt that somebody with my qualities could do a good job. But I got too much into the role and was never in class. I would be organizing events, concerts, and fundraisers and getting plenty of recognition and approval from fellow students and teachers. But none of this helped my grades

Sent Down

Much to my shame, at the end of the academic year, I failed to get the grades I needed to move up to the next class. I had to repeat the previous year's studies once again. I was the smartest guy there but there again, maybe I wasn't. I had not spent enough time in the classroom and I just didn't have the marks.

This hurt my Mum. I was the Pastor's son and I had to repeat a year of studies. She must have been so disappointed. I knew I had let her down, in my perspective she was dramatically ashamed of me and embarrassed that other kids were going forward and was left behind.

During this repeated year, I discovered that the teacher who I thought was being mean to me, was actually seeing my potential and trying to push me to do better and not settle for mediocrity.

So, for all of these reasons, I buckled down and put all my effort into my studies and soon made up for lost time. I did this for my mother, who was a huge positive influence on me. I thought of her as my source of life.

She taught me the value of good communication in any relationship. At the time, she was having a difficult time with my father. They were not talking. So instead, she talked to me. I am sure she must have been lonely but I enjoyed our chats. This might not sound like much, but to have the total attention of an adult who is interested in your thoughts and ideas, is very powerful when you are young. And I learned from it.

As I grew up, I got to the point where I would often be conflict with her. Looking back, I regret that. We expect our parents to be perfect and not make mistakes. But they are human just like the rest of us. Nobody is perfect.

There was a girl that I used to see in church. I was nine then in the early 1990s. I enjoyed talking to her. We had a phone in the house, although it wasn't used much. When my parents were working, I could spend hours on the phone chatting with her and thinking nothing of it. Later the phone bill arrived. It was huge. The equivalent of a couple of months salary. I was sitting in the car and heard him scream from inside the house. He came at me in the car.

I can still see his big hands coming toward me. He hit me everywhere. On my legs and on my back.

-"Are you crazy? Do you think we laugh and money comes? Do you think money grows on a tree? Do you know how much money you have spent on the phone?"

I had no idea that the phone was so expensive!

You guys are lucky now that there is WhatsApp and dozens of ways to communicate without paying a penny. Back then there was nothing but the phone.

By now, I saw my dad less and less. At a time when I needed the support that only a father can give, he was not in my life. I really craved having a male role model.

The thing that pushed him away from the family completely was when he made a terrible mistake with his finances. He was paid a lump sum which was for his retirement. To this day, I have no idea what happened, but suddenly the money was not there. It vanished. My mother was left with a mortgage and debts of over €180,000. I never knew why, but he then left and returned back to Uganda to stay with his mother. There was a lot of anger and a lot of sadness. I was now 23 and turning into a man. I was asking myself why life had to be so hard.

I thought to myself, why was it that I seemed to take one step forward, only to go fifteen steps backwards. I looked around at my friends who all seemed to be thriving. But here I was back at zero.

I had to make money and pay back the bills, take care of the household and take care of the church. So I found a job as a waiter and I worked hard.

I knew I couldn't properly move on with my life until I had found a way to forgive my father. I had to do a lot of work on myself. He may well have had reasons for what he did. For all I know, there may have been a positive intention in his mind. He might have thought what he did was the only option at the time. I just don't know. Sadly, I have not spoken to him for the last thirteen years and I am sad about that.

Chapter Five

Junior Summer Camping

In July 2001, I was excited to have been selected to go to the summer camp of a national youth group. It was to be held in a small village in the south of Italy, Ruvo di Puglia. I was looking forward to meeting my friends from all over the country, and to meeting new ones.

In those days, we didn't have Smartphones, Apps, games – or even the internet! We very much had to make our own entertainment. The photos we took then, are really special today.

These summer camps were to build leaders. Most of the people who attended are now leaders in their different spheres. We all had to cook, clean, and wash. For some, this was a new experience. I was grateful that my mom had taught me all these skills before.

Since the age of seven during the summer, when my parents were working, I had been responsible for taking care of my younger brother and to cook the food that my Mom had left out – complete with instructions as to what to do.

I was expected to warm up the food, wash the dishes, and clean the house: sweep and mop the floor. We did not have a hoover at that time. My mom had taught me to have fun while cleaning. We had even been taught to prepare and bake cakes at the weekends, this is also one of the main reasons why I love to cook. Those were lovely moments, quality time with my mom, I remember my parents could not afford to buy the GAME BOY, for those who know what it was, the most requested gadget from kids.

Coming back to the camping, few of my fellow attendees had been taught any of these skills, so we had to support them by multitasking. But it wasn't all work and after the chores were done, we had moments of sharing, singing, playing, reading, and praying.

During those ten days, I realized that I was better equipped and had stronger foundations than my mates. I never considered myself better, just that I had gone through some stuff and I had applied some things that they hadn't. I knew a bit more about real life.

During the camp, we had many moments of openness and sharing. Some of my mates started asking me questions and I found myself sharing what I knew. The organizers encouraged me to do this and to get me more and more involved.

After an intense month, the camp came to an end and we all had to go our separate ways. It had been an amazing experience and we still had a full month of holiday left before the new term started. I felt the need to keep in touch with all of the people I had spent so much time with. This was still the era for postcards, for stamps and letters. Emails were not yet so popular. So we all stayed in touch and shared our news and views.

I started sharing my experiences and what was helping me. I still remember I was going to the post office every day to post letters and buy stamps in advance. After the first 20-30 handwritten letters, I decided to make better use of my time and print them off on a computer. I did one newsletter about relationships and the other about academic results.

I shared the importance of being connected Spiritually as well as being connected to yourself. It may sound complicated or hard, but it wasn't and it isn't. I understood it from what my mom had taught me: our Spiritual connection cannot be separated from our personal connection because when we are all an expression of the Creator and we are fine in our imperfections.

Yes, you read it correctly: You Are Ok, Perfect in your imperfections.

I opened myself up and told them some of the mistakes I had made, and how I was constantly making wrong steps (trust me, I still make tons of mistakes), but it was ok, I was ok.

One of the girls, in particular, was constantly ashamed of herself and her body, she was too tall, according to her, and she did not have the perfect silhouette of a Victoria's Secrets model and therefore nobody would look at her. She had such a poor self-image. What I did with her was make her focus on the good things. She had an amazing smile, she was the best in the school and I told her that the opinions of others are not a verdict on her life. Now she is married and has three amazing kids.

Another was just angry with life because she had to do everything by herself. Her mother was absent and only her father was taking care of her, and she was looking after her brother and her small sister. In the letters we were exchanging, I helped her to shift her perspective and embrace the blessings life was offering her. It was a shifting game and it worked! She is married now and has an amazing boy.

Another boy from the camp, who I was corresponding with regularly, believed that school wasn't for him, and that he would just drop out of high school and find a job.

In my simplicity I told him that his words will determine what he will experience in the future so, we started together with a declaration process. At that time I didn't know that our Neuro system is wired with a connection between thoughts, vibrations, and words.

Well, we started changing the words he was using regarding school and specific subjects and it was this that turned him around. Changing his vocabulary changed his outcomes. He finished school and went to study and live in Australia.

These are just a couple of examples of the many people I coached as a result of the Summer Camps which I continued to go to until I was seventeen.

In the second summer camp, I also met one of the people whom I truly loved for so many years, until she got married in 2009. It was not until the last day of that summer camp that we realized we were liking each other. I remember we were traveling on a train listening to a song by Michael Jackson on our shared headsets. We continued repeating it again and again for the five hours of the journey. Finally, somebody was accepting me as I was, I didn't need to pretend, it was fine to be weird. It was good to be able to be who I was.

Ask yourself the question, how many of the qualities, values and traits that define you today can you trace back to your upbringing? I know that is very much the case with me.

When I was a small boy I spent my time between playing football and school. That was my life. It was who I was. I was carefree and enjoying the moment. My Mom saw a bigger picture for me and how I would need to change as I grew up, so she challenged me.

-"You are about to start a new academic year"
- "Now is the time to plan your life to make sure you have time to do everything." I needed a timetable. This was a new concept to me, I had never had to plan before. I just lived life as it came.
-"You need to know when you have to do homework, and all your other activities"

So she taught me how to plan and how to get organized. And I hated that at the time, but now I absolutely thank her.

Since I was a small kid, I was creative and disorganized. My room was not tidy at all, but in my untidiness, I could convince myself that I could find everything I was looking for. As I grew up though, I could see that lack of organization was becoming an issue. At one point my room was so bad that my mom refused to tidy it. She made me do it myself. Now, I don't blame her!

Being organized is not a skill I was born with and had to learn. It helped to understand the power of discipline and this was going to be essential in order to get through University.

That is not to say that I found it easy! Far from it. When I was young I wanted to do all those things that all my friends were doing. I wanted to party, hang out with friends, play football and live my life! I had the learn the hard way. We all do.

Discipline is choosing a temporary pain for longer pleasure. This is so difficult – at any age! We all want to be rewarded now not later. Pain can be put off.   So let me introduce the concept of anticipation.

Anticipation is the ultimate skill for both a business owner and also for an athlete. Anticipation is looking ahead to the reward you will receive by being disciplined. Making the task itself more important to you than a momentary pleasure of doing something else.

If you're able to anticipate the bigger reward attached to your goal, and sacrifice those smaller temporary pleasures that are tempting you, the big reward will be all the sweeter.

The secret is being disciplined for a purpose. You need to keep in mind the ultimate reward you will enjoy for being disciplined.

People who don't make it in life. make up excuses. People who do make it in life, make a plan, and they follow it up. You achieve the plan by being disciplined. When you have a plan and discipline you can afford to be flexible.

However, if you try to be flexible without a plan and with no discipline, you will be blown all over the place.

Throughout my school years, I have always had in the back of my mind a wish to become a politician. Maybe an Ambassador. I have always thought that the diplomatic service was where I wanted to end up. For this, I would need to have a degree in Law or Political Science. I looked into this in detail to see what I would need to do. In my view, Political science was too theoretical with very little practical work. If I was to make a career out of politics, I needed a mainly practical course.

Although I was only 16 at this point and in my third year in high school, I was pushing to go to the international school. To do this, I needed to get an average mark of 7.5 in all of my subjects. Unfortunately, I only made an average of 7.25. So, for the sake of a tiny 0.25, I didn't qualify. Naturally, I was very disappointed, but I didn't get angry because I realized that it was down to me and me alone. There was nobody else I could blame. This was probably the first time in my life when I didn't automatically point the finger at my parents, the school, or anybody else. I did an inventory of myself and realized that something had to change. If I wanted More, I had to become More. So I changed.

My motivation was to become a diplomat, or a lawyer. It would be really special for my Mom so I was doing all of this for her. I wanted to get into the International School and then into University.

I became obsessed with my studies. After football or athletics, instead of hanging about with my mates, I would go to the library and continue my studies. If I wanted a career in the diplomatic service this is what it was going to take. So I became focused on my studies and it paid off because, with the first exam I did for university, I achieved top marks.

With this focus, I now had to succeed with my law degree. I became quite idealistic. I was inspired by the television lawyer Perry Mason and his ability to talk with passion and eloquence to defend the weak and innocent and to give them a voice in a world full of injustice.I was also fascinated by the TV series Law and Order. I wanted to develop my skills as a speaker and an advocate. I wanted to be able to win arguments and present a case in front of a judge. So, I completely threw myself into my studies. I knew what I wanted to do.

At University, my first exam was on the legal system of the Roman Empire which I found fascinating. I would throw myself into every assignment and fill my mind with facts and quotes. I would practice the art of speaking eloquently in public and of presenting and debating an argument. I loved the 'David and Goliath' aspect of presenting a case and of winning justice for someone who could not defend themselves.

One of the subjects I loved was the history of the law. It was taught by a Professor who also happened to be the Dean of the University. Although I was averaging high scores in my exams, an average of 29.5 out of 30, I needed some extra marks and thought this course would be a good source of them. What I had not banked on was the fact that he didn't really like students. He marked my exam down to 27. I was furious. It was worth a far higher mark! So I rejected it. He then took offense. "Well Mister Nalocca it is a shame to ruin such a great score on your academic journey, if you reject it you will need to come back and sustain again the oral exam"

When I retook the exam he marked it even lower at 23 just out of spite. But I wasn't going to let him deflate my enthusiasm. I was unstoppable! So I accepted it as it had become a personal battle, no matter what I would have done he was not going to change his opinion. So I had to be the one to change.

Despite setbacks, I was getting a lot from University. I was learning how to be disciplined with my studies. I was learning how to manage my time. I also discovered the value of silence and studying in a peaceful environment. Before University I was not comfortable with my own company preferring to be out with friends and having a good time. Now I had learned the opposite and valued 'me' time and the power of silence. It was here that I started to appreciate the power of having music in my life.'

My Mom tried to introduce me to music at an early age but the music teacher she found was terrible. I had my keyboard at home and figured out how to play it by myself. My parents could not afford music lessons for me, and the teacher was not the best and very basic. I went online to download chords and learned what to do. As I got better, I realized that, for me, music was a way of recharging, when I was overwhelmed. That has stayed with me till today.

I believe music is the easiest way and fastest way to tap into a new dimension of consciousness. Not wishing to dive into the metaphysical, I believe there are different levels of consciousness. Music allows you to get into frequency, which takes you onto another plane. I love to play every type of instrument and, when I play, I realize that my brain is another place. When the music flows I don't need to think of the next step. It just happens automatically. Especially when I'm playing the piano and my fingers just know what to do. Music transforms and transports me and seems to 're-boot' my brain. I still have a lot I want to achieve in music, like to improve with my electric guitar and drums and finally learn to play the bass guitar.

Qualifying for University was a big thing. It is a time when everything changes. I had clear a goal and I knew want I needed to do. I was determined not to let distractions get in the way.

I felt the need to distance myself from my past and to become someone 'new' and 'cool'. I wanted to fit in, have friends, and be accepted but I was starting to run away from my calling. I decided that no one should know that I was speaking in church on a Sunday so I kept it a secret. None of my friends knew about it. I was afraid of what they might think.

I had chosen to fit in when I was called to Stand Out. I ran away from my gift.

My weekly routine started on Monday morning when I would return to my studies after working Friday, Saturday and Sunday in the restaurant. I was very focused and had no problem keeping my head down until I was interrupted by somebody knocking on the door. I was in a good routine. If I wanted a break, I would play music on my guitar. On Friday, Saturday and Sunday evenings, I would work to bring in money. Sunday morning was my favourite time of the week when I was happy and fulfilled. I was helping the kids, I was playing worship music, working with singers and other musicians, and helping others. This was my gift but I was afraid to talk about it.

I did have fun at university and made some good friends. I was the one that organized the parties and social events. I discovered that I was good at it. No wonder later on I got into the event industry, now I was not organizing University parties but massive self development events.

However, I needed to earn money to be able to live I did what many other students did, and become a waiter, cleaning tables and carrying glasses. In Italy, the main tourist season lasts from May to September. If you found the right place to work and applied yourself, you could make good money. That's what I intended to do. With my enthusiasm, positive attitude, and determination, I knew I could do well. If that meant starting at the bottom, then that's what I had to do.

I discovered that I was good at customer service and was known for having a great attitude. As a result, I did well with tips and caught the eye of the owners. I was given more responsibilities and it was not long before I became the manager, first of one venue and then two. It made a big difference to have money coming in.

I was also finding the time to become more proficient with music. It was a real escape for me to be able to drown out the voices, screaming in my head. Every time I needed to realign myself, I played music. I now have over five guitars, two sets of drums a piano, and four keyboards. My last purchase was bass guitar.

For me, music has become a health passion and a creative outlet. You see, we can meet our needs in a healthy or unhealthy way. Some people will meet their needs through drugs which is a way of evasion, and getting away from reality.

It is a negative activity that is damaging and not good for you, or the entire community.

&

In everything I was doing in and out of University, I was determined to prove to my Mum that I would succeed. However, there was a cloud on the horizon. I was putting every effort into the course and getting good marks but the more I learned about the workings of the legal profession the more I began to have doubts that this was for me.

It did not take me long to realize that my idealistic view of the law was not necessarily born out in real life. In many cases, money got in the way of ethics. Those who needed the protection of the law, but did not have the money, didn't get the justice they deserved. The more money you had, the more 'justice' you could afford. I started to ask myself if would I be prepared to compromise my integrity to win a case. Could I remain true to the beliefs and values that my mom had instilled in me? Was I moving in the right direction? Now I wasn't so sure anymore.

I was starting to see too many cases where Goliath had won over David when it should have been the other way around. This was not right.

I started to feel disappointed. The clarity I had about my studies started to become foggy. I had put my heart and soul into this profession, but I felt it was letting me down. This resulted in me losing my scholarship. It was the end of this road. I had no alternative but to leave the course and move back to live with my family.

Of course, I was sad that I didn't complete my master's degree but it was my choice because I didn't want to embark on a lifetime of compromising my integrity. My fellow students at that time have gone on to practice law and have made money. But to me, having More isn't just about money but also about contribution, purpose, and being true to myself. I know I made the right decision.

Whilst I didn't have a Master's what I had done was to give myself a Masters in Life. I graduated in being able to manage my state; in managing my disappointments; in being loving and compassionate; and also in forgiveness and letting things go.

In 2007, I was attending a personal development seminar. I always looked for opportunities to learn and grow. I watched the trainer skillfully manage a group of 30 people. I noticed how he kept everyone involved and gave them all opportunities to contribute and share. I was impressed with his technique. At that moment I could visualize myself doing that same thing in the future. I knew I had the skills and the confidence to stand on stage, but I still had doubts as to who would listen to me. I had baggage. I was still ashamed of the things my Dad had done and the fact that he had abandoned our family. There was a lot that I was holding back and couldn't share. I was stopped by that shyness and insecurity from opening up and being myself.

I started to study such inspirational speakers as Les Brown, Jim Rohn, and also Tony Robbins and how they can hold an audience of tens of thousands in the palm of their hand. I could start to see the direction my life might go in the future. But I wasn't there yet and in the meantime, I needed to earn money so I swallowed my pride and stepped down to a lower and less challenging role. I went to work, once again, in a bar as a waiter.

On the face of it, working as a waiter might seem like a demeaning job, but not for me. I had energy and enthusiasm and could help to make the customer experience a memorable one. As a result, I did very well on tips. It is never the job that counts, it is what you put into the job. I was prepared to put in more energy and time that the rest of my colleagues who were there just to do the minimum and make the minimum. Not me! This is the same attitude that brought me so far.

߸

I kept looking around for the next opportunity in newspapers and magazines because you never know what is around the corner. I saw a well-written and inviting advert for a commercial director which looked interesting. I had no idea what that meant, but I applied anyway. Much to my surprise, because I had no experience as a commercial director, I received a call inviting me for an interview. I dusted off my best blue suit once again. Who knows, this could be the one.

When I got there, I realized they were not in any way selective but were attracting and recruiting everybody. The other applicants were from all walks of life and all types of people. The offices were very upmarket, with expensive leather chairs and inspiring pictures on the walls of successful people like Muhammad Ali. There were posters about handling objections and motivational quotes. Everything has the smell of success.

I went into the boss's office. The smell of vanilla was everywhere. Then I saw it was coming from the tobacco in the pipe he was smoking. He was sitting on an impressive black leather chair, holding my resume. "I know you," he said. I recognized him as well. He used to be a famous boxer. I also remembered that he used to work as a bouncer in a restaurant where I had been a waiter. It was a small world. I thought to myself if a bouncer can have a luxury office and be a business owner, then there might be something I can learn here. He told me to come back tomorrow for an evaluation day. So I did.

The next day a group of us were sent out in a car to an area of the city. I thought we were going to the head office, but I quickly realized that this was a door-to-door selling job. I thought, well, I am here now. Let's not pre-judge, but let me give it my best.

In sales, it's not what you say; it's how they perceive what you say.

Jeffrey Gitomer

#It was the start of summer and very hot. I was in my suit and feeling very sweaty. I could see the tourist restaurants and bars starting to open for the new season. Tables were being washed and set up outside.

I went from door to door selling utilities without much success.

When I next saw the boss I challenged him:

-"I thought I had applied to be a commercial director."

He smiled. -"Welcome. This is the job. Are you hungry to earn money?" I was. I also didn't want to disappoint him, so I stayed. For two months, I didn't get any results. When I returned to the office at the end of the day, it was my colleagues who were ringing the sales bell and boasting of closing five contracts. I knew I was better than they were. Why wasn't it working for me? I had been to University, and I knew how to articulate an argument correctly and appropriately. I was speaking Italian better than a native. This was not making sense, my logical brain started to analyse and I got in a blame mood, blaming myself for what I had done, the decision of leaving my Uni, I thought I was better off before.

Have ever been in situation where you spend most of your time regretting the choice you made?

It was quite demoralizing, but I stayed with it. I started working on my script and my presentation and trying it out from one door to the next.

I worked out how to handle objections and how to close, but it still wasn't working.

I realized that everyone I went to talk to was busy. They were not expecting me, and I was an interruption to their day. I had to use all my enthusiasm and people skills to get a moment of their time. Every business I visited seemed to have a 'Sales Prevention Department' – someone whom you had to go through, like a PA or secretary, before you could talk to the decision maker. It was hard work. Then one day, I had a breakthrough and closed 20 contracts in one day. I knew then that I had cracked it.

Every day, my boss would drill into us, "It's all about attitude...positive attitude is all you need" At that time I just thought these were beautiful words just to be used in our sales environment.

Our boss was obsessed with those words: positive and attitude, positive and attitude. He was so obsessed with these words that they became our mantra, and if someone wasn't productive it was simply because he had a negative attitude.

Keep your face to the sunshine and you cannot see a shadow.

Helen Keller

As door-to-door salesmen, we used to meet every day at 7:30 in the morning in a tiny office. We would start with energetic music to get us into the right frame of mind, later on I realised it was a way of getting in 'state.' We had to rehearse the script, role-play a sales meeting with a client, and demonstrate that we knew the various stages of the sales presentation. This included the introduction, customer questions, handling objections, and closing the sale. We would take it turns going into the centre of the circle and playing the role of the sales agent of the client.

All the team would be watching us including a senior salesman and also the boss.

They were very focussed on the attitude we had during the presentation and how we came across. If he didn't like what he saw, he made us do it again and again. For many there, it was boring, but for me, this was a cornerstone in mastering my game.

The Amateur practices till he gets it right. The professional practices until he can't get it wrong

This time was the most important of the day. learning how to present and close. This was the time for me to be a sponge and to absorb all the knowledge that I could and master and refine my presentation skills. I was so obsessed with learning how to make the best presentation that I watched movies about salespeople and looked at the tiny details like how they held their pens, their posture and gestures while speaking.

In those 30-minute training sessions, everybody seemed so aligned, so positive, and so charged up, but as soon as the meeting was over and we had to go for breakfast, everyone seem to revert to their real selves. the "attitude, positive stuff" was over, which was a shame, and probably the reason not everybody succeeded.

Some reverted to "victim mode" and complained about how their sales were not as they wanted. Others complained about the territories they had been allocated and how some geographical areas were dead. Some complained that clients were rude to them and the names they were called. The rest just moaned about what wasn't going on in their lives, and about family, debts, and relationships.

If you have a positive attitude and constantly strive to give your best effort, eventually you will overcome your immediate problems and find you are ready for greater challenges.

Pat Riley

The senior leaders used to complain mainly about the product, the competitors, how the commission structure could be better if... and how the month could have been better if he had worked in a different area. Blaming everything and everybody but themselves.

From such an upbeat sales training event every morning, the contrast with what was actually going on in their heads was dramatic.

As the youngest sales agent and the only black guy, I wanted to master the game and I was asking always questions, questions, and questions.

"How could I handle this objection?
What should I have answered?
How come I couldn't manage that situation?
Why didn't I close?
What was missing?
How can I overcome such rejections? "

Before very long, some people in the team could not stand me and got tired of me asking so many questions. Why did I have to keep complicating things? They actually nicknamed me THE COMPLICATOR, simply because I was going into the details, I would not stop on the surface, I needed to get deeper and find the recipe of success.

They didn't realize that this was the only way to learn if you were serious about succeeding.

It wasn't easy but I was building my muscles. I had to learn to endure hard days and hard moments if I was going to have the good ones. I expected that I would have immediate results and I was in a rush to close the first sales, go into the office and ring the big bell.

I kept on trusting my boss and maintained a positive attitude and followed the process. Finally, on the 27th of June, the second last day of the month a business client made me sign my first multiple sales, 21 double sales in one day. Not only did I achieve my dream goal of ringing the big bell, but I also did the monthly record.

Now as I'm writing this, I just remembered that on that specific day I made a decision not to be sold to. Being sold to is when you buy into your customer's excuses for not buying.

Instead, I made the decision, not to listen to their excuses, but to keep on going with the presentation. I no longer chose to accept a "No" for an answer but to go on to close the sale. It was just a state of mind, my mind.

I remember this gentleman said: "Come back, let's do it next month this is the last day of June, it's Friday". I started to panic and visualize these 20 sales going away. I excused myself and called my boss for immediate support, he just told me: "Keep your stand and tell him that your commissions rely on these sales, offer him support on the paper work and make sure he signs. Regarding the rest, we will take care of it in the office" When I heard those words I felt charged and I believed I could make it happen, and so it did.

If it wasn't for my "positive attitude" I would have given up easily. In sales, I do not believe in a "Be back" – a client that says "I'll be back". They never will. If they do not buy when they have all of the information in front of them, they are just trying to let you down gently. A "Be back" is a No, but sugar coated.

People buy emotionally and justify it rationally. This is what I teach in my sales trainings.

When people say "No" to me, what they are actually saying is "No, I do not have enough information or reasons yet to say yes." You just need to provide them.

I grew up in a strong spirit-faith-oriented environment, the words " I can't, I'm not good at…" were not in our language, but as human beings, we get too familiar with situations, we take things and people too much for granted.

My mom taught me the right attitude and positive principles as I was growing up, but they faded along the way, clouded and covered behind a fog of routine and "possibility blindness".

I needed to be shaken up from the outside to stir up what I already had inside.

I had ups and downs and in the summer season, I got infected by the "season virus" that my colleagues seemed to catch. They had an excuse for everything: it was too hot and in summer it is hard to sell.

As a team, we were moving together as a group in different cities. Most of the members were finding ways of avoiding working and staying out of the heat. They would go to the pool then in the evening, go back to the office and complain that the area was dead, and impossible to close…

"Whether you believe you can, or you can't, you are right in both cases" Henry Ford.

They just didn't have sufficient belief in themselves.

Some days, I felt I was the only one working and, to be honest, I was pushing myself to maintain motivation. I was watching all my other colleagues doing as little as possible not putting in the effort. I can tell you, only now, that this was a tremendous blessing for me. More of that later.

Environment is stronger than you and your willpower.
For over two months my performances were in perfect line with the rest of the team. It wasn't what I wanted, but those were the results I was having.

At the daily sales trainings, I was always doing my best, putting all my effort into delivering the best presentation. The strange thing was that, in the 30 minutes in the office, I was giving my best. It was a safe environment, the boss was observing, and no one could criticize me or come up with their usual negative thoughts.

One day, the boss had the idea that, instead of going door to door, we should try selling over the phone. He wanted to set up a test in another city to see if it would work. He asked the leaders who would be best to do this try-out. They all said "Moses!". This was probably because they didn't want to do it themselves. Or get rid of the complicator for one full week.

The Boss said "Try to do the same presentations on the phone as you do face to face and count how many people you would really engage and close by phone."

So, off I went with my mobile phone and a phone book to conquer a new territory on my own. I adapted my presentation to make it work over the phone as he requested. I really wanted to make it work. After a week of making phone calls from morning to night, I had generated some results.

The Boss and his partners came to meet me and asked me a load of questions. They looked at the script I had created and accepted it. As a result of this trial, they decided to open their first call centre.

It opened on the 25th of November 2008. I believed that I would be made a director and would manage it. But this didn't happen.

-"You are too young to be the director," they told me. Instead, they made me the team leader with forty staff for me to manage. Of course, it was a great opportunity, but I was very disappointed and felt denied something I had created was given to another director.

I hid my feelings and set out to prove them wrong by putting all my energy and focus into making it a success. I was not only training everyone, but I was also on the phone from nine in the morning till nine at night and producing results. Everyone else just did a half day. I was determined to prove that the boss had made a mistake. In addition, I wanted to prove to myself what I was capable of.

The call centre was a huge success. Then in 2010, the company decided to open an even bigger call centre in another city. I naturally thought that with all the success I had created in the first centre, it would now be my turn. My moment.

But the new call centre wasn't going to be my turn or my moment to be a director.

They gave it to somebody else and made me team leader again.the director. I was devastated.

Have you ever been in a situation where you always seem to be the second choice? I started to question everything.

Is it my colour?
Is it my young age?
Is it because I don't come from a business family?

However, I put all these doubts to one side and looked at the opportunity instead. I went on to repeat the success I had achieved in the first call centre, but even better. I was good, and I knew it. I put my head down and kept working. Once again, I trained and motivated my team.

As always, I led by example and always managed to sell more than everyone else. Then history repeated itself and, one year later, they started to plan to open a third centre. This time I had no expectations. If they don't make me a director, I was going to leave.

I even started to look around for other opportunities. Enough is enough. But I was wrong.

They did offer me a directorship in the biggest and most technically advanced call centre that you could imagine. I had a team of 144 reporting directly to me. It was a massive task for me to manage them all. My phone never stopped from dawn to dusk. The results we achieved were terrific. Sometimes we think that God's delays are denials, looking backwards I'm so grateful for those delays because I was able to develop my leadership skills. Sometimes you need to be careful on what you ask. To be honest it was not because I was young or my colour. If I would have become a director earlier I would have failed miserably, because I was lacking some skills that were essential to my future career. When you ask for MORE, sometimes it will take time because you are not ready.

Two years after my promotion, the boss called me into his office. -"I need you for a new role". I need your social skills, I need your management skills. I want to give you a new role." Immediately I felt defeated. Had I not proved myself enough? Had I not been responsible for growing three call centres from scratch and generating a massive turnover for the business?

-"We have become a victim to our success." We are generating a huge quantity of orders, but we have a 30% cancellation rate." So for every thousand orders, we were closing, we were not

getting paid on three hundred. That percentage was far too high and a big profit leak. He wanted me to head up a new Quality Control department. There would be a team of girls who were not working on making sales but on changing the fact that we were losing 300 sales every day.
It didn't excite me.

I felt it was a demotion, a punishment. Suddenly all my past fears and inadequacy feelings surfaced again. It was one thing was to be a director of a call centre, the level of significance and importance was high. But and now they want me to be a director of quality control? What is that??

I had yet to realize the importance of the role. I would become the main overall director, I would have a company car, a phone and I would be given expenses with a personalized company bank card. Moreover, I was the one who had to go the meetings with our main suppliers and present the scripts and recordings of our calls in order to argue potential cancellations, negotiate the cooling periods and cancellations policies. Now it was starting to look better.

So once again, I started from the bottom. I had to learn a new role and then train a team to control the quality of the sales people and reduce the number of cancellations and credit rejections. I accepted the challenge and threw myself into it, with excellent results, in fact, better than the company expected. With a team of only sixteen girls, we went from having 30% cancellations to only 5%. A huge improvement in the company profits.

At this time, I started to pay the price for the long days I was working, the amount of travel I was doing to visit the call centres, suppliers, and my lack of exercise and eating take-away meals on the run. I was starting to experience burnout. I was not looking after myself and putting my job first.

My fellow directors strangely didn't seem happy that we have achieved such an increase in profits:

-"We would have been quite happy with an improvement of 15% to 20%. To achieve 5%, you have had to reject many more customers, even if the quality of their business might have been poor. And this is costing us money."

It seemed to me that they had missed the point. They knew the price of everything but the value of nothing.

I asked them, "Would you rather be paid on 750 contracts out of every thousand, or would you like to be paid on 950?" Their answer told me that I was not being appreciated and that it was time to move on.

They were not happy at all that I made it, they started to see me as an enemy. In a childish way they started putting obstacles, delaying my requests, ignoring my orders. I started to blame myself, but I realised it wasn't about me, they could not stand the successful results. I shared this with my mom and she told me one thing that became a cornerstone in my life:

"Successful people do not spend time criticising others, they are happy to see them succeed"

For a while I ignored them and continued to do my part with more determination and drive.

In six years I helped the company go from zero to a projection of 20 million in revenue by the end of the 2014. Massive achievement, yet in me something was starting to stir up: what is my next level? I want MORE.

It was time to have a conversation with the owner of the company. When I set up the appointment I was nervous and yet confident.

"So here we are, in the new task you gave me 1 year and a half ago I reduced from 30% to 5% the cancelations and increased the collections. What is my new challenge?

What other opportunities are out there? Where else can I add value?"

"Well Moses, there is not much to say. You went way beyond what we expected. Nothing else to say or add."

"Ok, so is there a chance to grow and do more?
"Moses at the moment you are number 3 in the organization, you manage the entire business, what else do you want? There is no more space, because that means you will have to take my place."

-"Thank you if that's the case then I hand in my 60 day notice and start to plan the handing over to my successor"

I did it. It was painful to resign and lose all of the perks and salary, but I knew it was the right moment.

I invited the owners and the partners for a goodbye dinner and thanked them for the great opportunities and experience learned in the journey of 6+years.

Throughout my time there, the one thing I learned was that I was the only person that I could rely on. I had now developed a powerful set of skills. I had proved to myself what I was capable of and knew I could transfer those skills anywhere.

Chapter Six

A New Start

It was a huge leap to leave the call centre business and the culture of a big organization. I was used to having all the infrastructure in place and having people and departments I could call on for support.

When you start up a new business, everything is down to you. There are so many things you take for granted, the simple things like phones and IT. When I opened my own sales agency, I went from having a structure, a team, and marketing in place, to walking into an empty room and starting from scratch.

What I did have was the confidence of having built a huge organization for somebody else. If I can do it for them, I can do it for myself. I certainly missed having a team to work through, imperfect though they were.

So, if things were to be, they were up to me. I stepped back in time to the days when I started in the call centre business, and went door-to-door once again, offering a range of sales tools and services to companies. These were delivered through a small group of outsourcing partners. I had no problem walking through any door to sell. I was bombproof.

I looked at the marketplace and saw a need for a structured sales process. So I went off to sell it in the biggest cities to the largest companies. I was not going to be accused of thinking small!

What I quickly learned is the big value of having a back office in support. Selling, follow-ups and administration, and all vital functions. One person can't do it all.

I also needed to be working with people who shared my vision and are not held back by thinking small. My mission was to be working with the giants, the big mall owners, and the multi-nationals. I knew that I was a nobody, but I also know that, with what I had developed and the experience I had, I could make a real difference in their businesses.

Think big work small. While I was searching for companies to offer my services, one small young company approached me, a marketing agency.

Sales is the one thing common to every business. There isn't one that does not need more sales. I discovered that it takes the same amount of time and effort to sell to a small business as it does to sell to a large one, so I headed for where the big numbers were. I saw myself as a salesman adding value to a company as an expert in that area. I could train a team to become more proficient in making sales. I could help with sales strategy, I could manage the sales process.

What I quickly found was that some people are more scared of success than of failure. Failure is a comfort zone of blame that is easy to share around. Success is demanding, It raises momentum. Not everyone is ready for it. Somewhere between success and failure is a limbo where you keep your job by keeping a low profile. This is not a space I wanted to occupy.

I remember working with this marketing agency. I saw the bigger picture and started to get in touch with the biggest chain of malls in Italy, I don't know how I managed to get to sit with the Marketing manager, but I did. I borrowed my girlfriends car and travelled three hours in my nice black suit with my lucky blue tie.

They say 90% of success is showing up, and that what I did. On that occasion I did not conclude a deal but the experience boosted my confidence. The next stop was reaching out to the competition: Auchan group and the giant Nestle, both headquartered in Milan. For these big appointments the owners of the marketing agency came with me in Milan, but were afraid to sit in the meeting so I was once again alone with the Giants.

I was satisfied and proud of myself, I managed once again to create new opportunities and I was playing the game with the big players. On the way back home we had a discussion in the car. The owners asked me to scale down.

"What? I'm here providing you great opportunities and opening new doors and you want to scale down, stay local, and just work with the small shops in the neighbourhood?" As a matter of fact, that's what they wanted.

For some of the companies I was working with or approaching, my vision of their success was larger than their own. We were not speaking the same language, and we certainly didn't share the same values or vision. Success demands momentum and commitment.

Richard Branson once said that

When there is an opportunity, take it up and then figure it out.

His success in many markets and businesses proved him right. That was certainly my philosophy.

No matter what the opportunity, I believe you will be recognized and rewarded not by what <u>you</u> do, but by what you cause to happen. You can only do that by working with people. You can't do it all yourself. The people you work with need to share your vision, your values, and your work ethic. You cannot assume that they are thinking what you are thinking no matter if they say "Yes". It is not what people say, it is about what they do.

The partners I was working in the sales agency were disappointing me with their small vision. They worried about coping with success, and their fear was holding them back, and also the business. Eventually, because our vision was not aligned, I ended up closing the company.

I failed again.

Disappointing though this was, I learned a huge amount in the process and came out of it stronger, rather than weaker. Some lessons are hard to learn.

Every adversity, every failure, every heartache carries with it the seed of an equal or greater benefit.

Napoleon Hill

I think in most relationships
that have problems,
there's fault on both sides.
And in order for it to work,
there has to be some common
ground that's shared.
And it's not just one person
making amends.

Steve Carell

Chapter Seven
Shared Values

At this time I had been in a relationship for some time. Everything was going well but there were many things where we were not aligned, and led to rows. Some of them were big. She was not one to take risks and needed the security of being in a comfort zone with a predictable life around her.

It is a late evening of September 2014 and as I am driving going towards the shop to pick her up I can see the palm trees and I can feel the cool breeze of the Fresh air on my arm as the left arm is out of the window. As I approach the shop I have mixed feelings On one hand I'm so proud of the day I have had. On the another hand I'm worried of what I have to expect.

She closes the shop and released her long brown hair. She's is beautiful. She approaches the car andshe gets in, -
"Hi babe how was your day?
"Good how was yours? Did you do it?

Did you leave your place of work?

"Yes I did."

"OK now you can apply for an ordinary job I'll be working in the shop and you can find another job and together we can move on building our family."

"Babe we already had this conversation I'm not going to work in a factory or be an ordinary person I'm pushing for the best for both of us and for our future family."

"Everybody else has an ordinary job, why not you? Other families are living with this type of income and they're living a wonderful, comfortable life. Why do you need to search for more? Why do you need to have more?"

When I left my previous company, she saw this as an opportunity for me to move into the safety of a manual job in a factory doing nine to five. She didn't recognise my achievements in either coaching or in sales. She didn't understand that my search for More, was to bring more into our family and our lives, not a selfish quest for material things.

We were in the car and she is sitting there with angry eyes screaming at me. At that moment I realised that we were not aligned. I was searching for more, so I could give more to my future family. She was settling for stability. Don't get me wrong, I love stability too.

But I want stability in a healthy way. We're all meant to progress to move forward, not to regress or stay in one place.

That was a turning point for me in my life because I realised the importance of being aligned and on the same page with the person who's close to you.

Now, being aligned doesn't mean that there will not be disagreements. I'm not saying that. I'm just saying that I was searching, I was studying I was pursuing more in life, so I could give more to my family. And she wasn't seeing it that way. She was seeing what I was doing as a waste of time.

She wanted me to live a life where I had no challenge. I could never settle for less when I was made for More. Much More.

"Babe this is not what I want for us and I'm sorry we have total different visions I believe we should take some time and I can go to my mom as we said to our situation"

"Well it's up to you. You can leave"

Sadly we parted after weeks of constant arguments and fights.

As she dropped me to my mum's place, I feel I've failed again. I feel I failed with the most important person in my life. And now I have no choice but to go back to my mum's place.

As I opened the door there, I felt as if I have my tail between my legs. I felt beaten up, sad, and angry and yet I had a sense of comfort being back at home. Over the following weeks I tried to get in touch with her but she wouldn't take my calls. I expect that now she's too just angry to talk to me.

Had I communicated in the wrong way? I wasn't sure. Certainly I was not willing to compromise on my dreams or my desire and passion to search for more to be more to give more. Now I'm back, full circle, in my Mamas place with no girlfriend, no job and no direction going forward.

The only comfort that I had was listening to my personal development audio tapes. In one of those days I heard Les Brown saying:-

"When you fall make sure you fall on the back so you can keep your head high and have the final strength to raise up and move back again."

A couple of months later, she sent me a message. "Well, have you made your millions yet? Have you made the money that you wanted? She taunted. Have you found what you are looking for?"

The sad truth was that I hadn't. I was completely broke. I was back living with my mother in her house and abiding by her rules. I was demoralized and stopped looking after myself. I was getting out of shape and not myself. Things had to change. I had to change. So I did.

I started by getting back into my fitness regime and running for an hour every morning. I had become so skinny partly because I was punishing myself. Inside of me, I was feeling that if it's not painful enough, I am not making enough progress. This was the limiting belief I was working on.

I got back in the habit of running in the hills around the town in the fresh air. If I was honest, I was out there hoping to run into my ex-girlfriend but that didn't happen. I had my headset on and I was feeding my mind with motivational audios. I had to feed my mind as well as my body.

For five long months I was without a job but searching and applying for one every day. I kept up my daily running sessions and was getting back to my original fitness. I was listening to such greats as **Tony Robbins, Jim Rohn, Les Brown and Zig Ziglar.** However, it was **T Harv Eker** with his book, **The Secret of the Millionaire Mind** containing stories of people who had started with nothing, or less than nothing, and had rebuilt themselves by applying a new philosophy about money. Many of them were just like me and were jobless with only pennies to their name.

Despite that, I followed the advice in the book and started saving right away.

Reading is to the mind what exercise is to the body.

Joseph Addison

It wasn't just a matter of saving, the major issue was how to generate money. Part of the philosophy in the book was that. As an employee you had a cap on earning money. As a business owner you have no limit on how much you can earn. So I started thinking about going back into business on my own.

As Robert Kiyosaki teaches in ***"The Four Quadrant Flow"***, as an employee you are trading your time for money. With self-employment, you think you are managing your time but you are still trading something in exchange for money. As a business owner you have systems and teams working for you.

As an investor, money is working hard for you. This was the moment that I started studying business from another perspective. I wanted to be a business owner or an investor.

I had noticed something, by observing other people. A lot of business owners when the company fails, their first reaction, when looking to start again, is to do so from a lower position on the ladder, which helps to rebuild their self-esteem.

Looking back, this is what I did when my business failed, and when I broke up from my toxic relationship. I downgraded myself and went out to look for a job far below the business owner I had been. I even changed industries and went back to working in the hospitality industry in a restaurant. I went back to working weekends, and to serving at weddings. It paid well.

Can you imagine at this point what my mindset was like?

At that time I was earning €90 per day and this increased when I was able to work Friday, Saturday and Sunday. It was easy work. I enjoyed working with people and I was putting my free time to good use. It helped me pay for fuel, phone and food.

What didn't help my mindset was that all my friends had turned their back on me. My ex-girlfriend told everyone her side of the story and everyone believed her. They all had expectations that we were going to evolve into a relationship and were hostile to me because they though the breakup was my fault.

But it is difficult to live with toxicity. She couldn't understand why I was driven to be a success and why I was always looking for more. Her ideal life was to be one of the herd and to be satisfied with the ordinary.

Toxic people defy logic. Some are blissfully unaware of the negative impact that they have on those around them, and others seem to derive satisfaction from creating chaos and pushing other people's buttons.

Travis Bradberry

One day, when I was serving at a wedding, I noticed to my horror that one of my past employees was at the event. I froze! She had been one of a pool of secretaries that reported to me.

-"Hi! How are you doing?" She was looking at me up and down and I could read her thoughts. In her mind she was saying "Well you used to be my boss, always in an expensive suit and tie and driving fast cars. Now here you are dressed as a waiter and serving guests at a wedding. What happened to you?". It got worse. There were a number of my old school friends from High School on other tables close by.

How would you feel if it was you?

Have you ever wished, at a moment like this, that you had an identical twin that could have been there in your place?

At that moment I felt totally humiliated. I even asked the head waiter if I could look after other tables, far away from them. I just wanted to hide as if I had stolen something from them or as if I owed them something.

This was a huge lesson for me because I realised that, even if I had failed, even if I had lost my position, I wasn't stealing. I wasn't selling drugs. I had not turned into a criminal or looked for an easy road. So what did I do? I swallowed my pride and humbly went on serving. I knew this was a setback, but I also knew I had the strength and determination to bounce back. I was only 30 and I had my whole life in front of me. I just needed to speed up and run faster.

Success is how high you bounce when you hit bottom.

George S. Patton

I wanted success quickly with the same speed that they serve you in McDonalds! Make it large – and make it now!

I do know that there are many people who work for twenty or thirty years, and never become millionaires. But there again, there are those that do. What is it that they are doing differently?

I needed to know. Maybe the answer was already inside me. I started to go to training events to find out.

As I was in Italy at the time, I found a personal development seminar in Milan. Then I found another one in Rome. I realised that the speakers were speaking in Italian and were just repeating what they had heard from an English or American speakers in the UK. Then it occurred to me that I needed to hear the original not a copycat, and for that I needed to go to London.

My Mom is old school and to her, being successful is about studying, getting a degree, finding a job and building a family. She did not understand that my vision was different. I wanted to build a business and be in charge of my future. Although that had not worked out the way I had planned up till then, I wasn't going to be beaten! The only normal job I had was that of a waiter. Everything else had been on commission or on payment for results.

By now I had started a new business with a friend who has just graduated and had a passion for marketing. We heard about IOT, "The Internet of Things". It is a bit like helping your washing machine have a conversation with your fridge. It was brilliant, but nobody understood it then. And probably not now either! What we wanted to do was to use the IOT technology to give a new marketing tool for businesses. My business partner moved to London, to learn English. I was still in Italy, running the business and working weekends at weddings.

Yet I was searching for a smarter way to speed up the process.

At this point, I was devouring a book a week. I was hungry. At the same time I was feeling humiliated staying at my Mom's house. I was fighting with my demons.

Have you ever been in a situation where you have mixed feelings?

On one side I was fighting, pushing. On the other side I was totally embarrassed.

The Universe responded and brought to my attention a seminar in Monte Carlo. Little did I know that this event would point me in a new direction that would completely change my life.

It opened my eyes to the world of Life Coaching. It was the perfect way of using all the skills and experience I had accumulated. More on this later. What I do know is that whenever I had a need for knowledge or inspiration, the opportunity came along. It was up to me if I turned up to hear it.

You will only succeed if you turn up. Be there!

Before confirming my presence in Monte Carlo at an event called "Strategies for Coaching", I spoke with my Mom and after a long while, I managed to have a calm conversation. My mom is an interesting character. She gave me plenty of space in my lowest moment. She supported me in my series of interviews and business ventures.

-"Moses as you are spending so much time in London, why don't you see if you can find something over there?
Maybe your friend could find you a job over there as well?"

Wow! This was an answer. I always felt guilty when my work took me away from supporting her. She needed my help and support. I also had my duties in the church and the community, so moving to London would be a big step.

What has been stopping you so far from moving forward?

What had been stopping me was the fear of not being loved. Sub consciously, I had taken over the role of my Dad. I had to be the one to support and sustain the family. Now with my Mom suggesting that I go to London, I felt relieved.

I confirmed immediately my presence in Monte Carlo, packed my stuff, my two suits, three shirts, my smart black shoes and a pair of trainers. I was ready for anything! There were three of us travelling together by car. I used part of my last income from working in the restaurant the previous weekend and paid my share of the expenses for the four nights.

On the 4th of December I paid British Airways €42 to get me from Nice to Gatwick. My friend met me at the gate and told me I should have gone to Stanstead which would have been closer. You can't win them all!

He also allowed me to sleep temporarily in his flat in the bedroom of his two children. I remember the bed was so small, my feet would stick out at the bottom. He suggested that I paid him £400 a month whilst I was looking for a permanent place. I was grateful for that solution but it was not ideal so I had to look for an alternative as soon as possible.

Once again, I knew I could make money by working hard. It didn't take me long to be able to earn enough to move out into a flat of my own. My goal was to earn enough money each month to pay my rent, pay for my phone, and have enough money to buy a ticket for the next seminar. I had a plan!

One big point I learned was that,

We often overestimate what we can achieve in an hour or a day, but underestimate what we can achieve in the next three to five years.

Then I heard that Tony Robbins was coming to London. This was the one event I had been waiting for. It was a wonderful chance for me. I contacted the organisers, Success Resources and asked them how much the tickets were. The cheapest was £800. At that time this was a lot of money for me. I asked if I could pay in installments — and they kindly agreed! So my focus was very clear, to earn enough money to pay for my ticket in time before the event. I worked out that I could afford to pay the last installment three days before the event. Believe me I was motivated!

I worked out my income to the penny. From my first salary of £900, £400 of it went on rent The remaining £500, 250 went on paying towards the Tony Robbins ticket. What was left was for food, phone and transport, but I was happy. I was getting back in the game and that was what counted.

In my day job working in the bar, I was always trying to get any extra shift that was going. I wasn't where I wanted to be, but it was helping me to achieve my plan step by step. After a couple of months I switched roles and began to work as a waiter on the floor. I knew that waiters always get tips which you don't get behind the bar.

In fact, I quickly proved that I could easily double my wages this way. This enabled me to help my personal development by attending more trainings and seminars. I learnt so much!

If you change the way you look at things, the things you look at change.

Wayne Dyer

It is not what we get.
But who we become,
what we contribute...
that gives meaning
to our lives.

Tony Robbins

Chapter Eight
The UPW Experience

I t is April and a couple of days before the event **Unleash the Power Within** and I'm so excited! My roommate and I were planning to offer accommodation to at least another five attendees, a bit like an AirBnB, to make some extra cash. We were only some ten minutes from the venue, Excel London, where there would be some 10,000 people in attendance. I was thrilled to be one of them.

To be honest I had been panicking a little bit because I had only managed to pay the final installment of my ticket exactly three days before the day of the event. I didn't receive confirmation of my last payment until I called them the day before. A close call!

On the day of the event, I woke up early in the morning at 6am. It was going to be a long and exciting day! With 10,000 people in the queue to get in I had to get there in plenty of time.

As a reached the venue with my roommate and our temporary lodgers, we could hear the music and the vibrations from outside. The excitement was building!

Nothing could have prepared me for the impact of walking into the room. The sight of ten thousand excited people is a sight to be seen! The music was booming, there was a full grid of moving lights that you would expect to see at a stadium gig. On stage there was a troupe of twenty synchronized dancers performing an energetic routine. This was no ordinary seminar, this was in a whole new league!

Suddenly the music paused. A commanding voice filled the darkened room. "Ladies and Gentleman, please welcome on stage, Mr Tony Robbins!" The room exploded.

I can barely contain the tears of excitement. I had worked many long hours to save up for my ticket. Finally, I'm here and training with the greatest personal development trainer on earth. This had been one of my most important life-goals for many years. I was going to get the most out of this moment. For the next four days I choose to be like a sponge and absorb everything every single word. I took extensive notes which I knew would take me at least a month to go through and harvest the value from them. It would be as good as attending the whole event again!

Even today I spend time at least once a month going through my notes of that incredible event remembering in my heart and in my mind the experienced emotions the failings and everything that I learned in those days. Even today I still use what I learned over those four days

For me, my biggest breakthrough on the first day was how to deal with my fears and the limiting beliefs that were stopping me. Tony built us up with enthusiasm and excitement from 12:00 noon till about 10 pm. What amazing energy he had! Then just as we thought the day couldn't get any better, he announced a Firewalk!

Walking on fire is such a cathartic experience and this was my first time. When you look at those burning coals, they are very real and very hot. We have all grown up to be frightened of fire, and for a very good reason. Your brain instinctively tells you to stay away! To do a fire walk you have to override your natural instinct for self-preservation. You need to have a very good reason to do a fire walk. I did. And I couldn't wait!

I knew it would be a life-changing experience. I was determined to burn the old Moses and for the new Moses to rise from the ashes. So determined I was that, after doing it for the first time, I broke the rules, joined the queue again, and did it three times instead of once. I wasn't going to take any chances about getting rid of the old Moses!

The meaning of walking on fire was to go beyond your own limits. When you can walk on fire, what else can you do that your limiting beliefs were stopping you from achieving?

For me, walking on fire meant the chance, the possibility and the ability to overcome my fears. It took courage to take that first step but for me it completely delivered. I become an 'Overcomer'.

The higher your energy level, the more efficient your body The more efficient your body, the better you feel and the more you will use your talent to produce outstanding results.

Tony Robbins

Tony Robbins uses a specific technique to get you into the right 'state of mind' to take a specific action. He does this by using a combination of his words, his energy and moving your body. You need to tap into energy to achieve anything!

I use this technique for myself and also when I work with business owners or elite athletes. I used it to get me into the right head space before attempting anything important – like the fire walk. With that I needed to be in a state of total certainty and total focus.

That state of total certainty, of knowing who I am, knowing what I can achieve, and knowing what I will do and, no matter what, knowing I will achieve my goal. This is the state I was in before stepping forward to do the firewalk.

I had to overcome all those negative thoughts that were holding me back

The first one was my scarcity mindset. When I first walked on fire, I choose to give up on my scarcity mindset and walkthrough to abundance. I chose to walkthrough to creating the power of adding massive value. I decided that, from that day on, money would not be a problem for me. From that moment on, I would have not worry anymore about money.

I wasn't allowed to do a second fire walk but I was so determined that I did it anyway. This time I had a new focus. I wanted to breakdown all of my fears and then completely open myself. I wanted be in a state where I was open to receive Love and also able to share it. Love is the greatest gift.

Later in the evening, having helped the huge queue to share this same experience. There was a gap. It was my cue to take a third fire walk. I looked around and nobody was going to stop me.

This time I focussed on my future. I was going to be the author that wrote on the blank pages of my life ahead. Nobody else was going to write down my future. I had to take charge of what lay ahead in my life. I stepped forward onto the red-hot coals and took charge of my future. And it felt good! My life was going to be on my terms, nobody else's!

I cannot help but feeling emotional. The whole experience was unbelievably powerful. I had never had this sort of experience before. I was a different person without any doubt. The fears I had had, the lack of direction, the feeling of being lost, had all vanished. I felt purposeful and determined. The old Moses was definitely in the ashes I had left behind.

As I walked home after the final night with my feet dirty and still covered in ashes. In all of the three fire walks, I didn't burn myself at all. Actually, I didn't feel a thing.

I barely slept that night. The excitement and the level of energy was so high.

I now realised that, with all of the excitement, during the first hour of the first day, I had lost my voice. I had hardly noticed! Finally I was in the right place. Finally, I was in a place of power. I had shifted my identity and now was looking at myself as a Fire Walker. I was empowered, I was ready, I was hungry. So what could stop me now? Nothing.

What we can or cannot do, what we consider possible or impossible, is rarely a function of our true capability. It is more likely a function of our beliefs about who we are.

Tony Robbins

The second day of UPW I arrived even earlier. Once again I was queuing to get in. The ticket that I had saved up for was the cheapest ticket in the house. I was at the the back of the room yet I didn't feel any difference. I could clearly hear and see everything on the many screens that were there. All I was focused on was every word, every nugget of gold that was shared on stage. I was a sponge. absorbing everything that I could during the event.

Day two hit the ground running with Joseph McLendon III.

Joseph McClendon III is one of the most sought-after Ultimate Performance Specialists in the world. His unique techniques rapidly trigger the personal change that effectively moves you to take more consistent action and go Further and Faster with your personal and business achievements.

Joseph has delivered hundreds of workshops, coaching sessions, keynote addresses, seminars and training programs, one-on-one therapeutic intervention, and has presented to well over three million people around the globe. His remarkable ability to go straight to the core of the challenge and effect rapid change makes him a unique commodity in business, health, and wellness, and personal improvement. And right now he was in front of me on stage. What an amazing opportunity!

Now, I keep myself fit and I believe that I have great reserves of energy, but compared with Joseph, I was a couch potato! At that time of the event, Joseph McLennan was 65 and he spent the entire day on stage standing, jumping and speaking with such boldness and energy it was electrifying!

Day Two gave me the opportunity to take stock of the huge amount I had learned on Day One, and to start applying it to my own situation. There was a lot to think about!

I had to look honestly at my present reality and see how I could reframe it to make the changes I needed to moving forward

I had to get clarity on what my goals were; clarity on where I was going; and clarity on what was stopping me from getting there. It was going to be a deep dive and. what I would learn surprised me.

It is in your moments of decision that your destiny is shaped.

Tony Robbins

I know that I can be very focused when I am working on achieving a goal. I will work from the very start of the day and often work late into the evening. Not surprisingly, when I am in that mode I can often become so immersed that I can cut myself off from others and be selfish. I learned that sometimes I should have taken things easier, given myself more breaks and reminded myself to be a little more human. When you are too harsh on yourself, it is easy to forget to look after yourself.

I kept myself under pressure, and under more stress than was healthy. This was good to learn.

I learned that you actually achieve more when you give yourself to time to recover Pacing yourself gives your brain more opportunities to think ahead. You should always leave space for a little lightness or humour with those around you. It helps them as well as you. So give yourself a break at regular intervals and stop beating yourself up!

Day Three was equally powerful for me. Tony was back on stage and took us through an exercise to help us release those things in our past that no longer serve us in moving forward.

For me, I was still carrying bitterness and anger toward my dad. I could not shake off all the negative memories that I had of him. They kept on circulating in my head and stopping me from moving on. I realised that unless I could find the courage to address this, it would ruin the rest of the event for me and I would not heal.

I realised that, over the years I had been taking one step forward, but then by hanging on to my anger and negative thoughts, I had then gone fifteen steps backward. This could not continue. I could this continuing to clinging on to these negatives for years into the future, unless I took action now. Something I should have done a long time ago.

Holding on to anger is like grasping a hot coal with the intent of throwing it at someone else; you are the one who gets burned.

Buddha

I summoned up my courage, there and then, and for the first time, I forgave him. Immediately, I felt a weight lifted off my shoulders. Tony had helped me to release all of that baggage and my heart felt lighter

In that one moment I also reached out to my late brother, Joshua who was never far from my thoughts. I told him how much I loved him and how much I missed him. I cried, oh yes, I cried. but these were tears of relief, they were tears of joy, they were tears of freedom, they were tears of liberation. This one act of forgiveness towards my father enabled me to truly connect myself to my deepest heart. I was a changed man.

Many people believe that bottling up your emotions means you are strong. I disagree.

By not coming to terms with your feelings you are damaging yourself and delaying the possibility of getting closure. You get stuck, and cannot more on.

The Forth Day of UPW was the day of Vitality. I pride myself on my fitness, although this was not always the case. However, I quickly realised that, even though I was young, I wasn't taking care of my body to the extent that I needed to. If I wanted to achieve to my full potential I needed to make my body my priority. My body was my biggest asset that I had, and the only asset that I was able to manage and control directly.

A special moment

The biggest thing I learned about Tony over those four days is his generosity with his time. The high level of energy he gave on stage over those four days, was enormous. At the end of each day, he would have been forgiven in leaving the venue and going back to his hotel to rest.

At the end of day Three, it was 11.30pm. The event was over and everyone left the building on a high to go home. However, something told me to stay. After about thirty minutes, Tony came back out with a towel over his shoulders and sat down on the edge of the stage. The few people there moved to the front so I did the same. Tony sat there and spoke from the heart. A wonderful thing to experience.

He shared with us one of his major failures in life. At that time, he was traveling around the world wanting to concentrate on his speaking and his performances. So he delegated the running of his business to somebody else. Sadly, this person nearly led his business to bankruptcy.

He also spoke about his divorce and how his ex-wife wanted him to leave the island in Fiji, which was his refuge and his secret place to recharge.

He spoke with such a high level of humanity and understanding that I felt as though he was talking directly to me.

He spoke about his divorce from somebody he loved from a very young age. Then he spoke about his failure where he almost went bankrupt and he had to lay off his team. He shared the story of him going from $31,000 in profit in one year, to going above $1,000,000 in the next.

Never mind the money, but what I saw was the possibility and the opportunity for me to turn my life around and for me being able to achieve more. Much more.

Finally, one of the biggest take-aways I experienced over the four days was just one sentence. This has become my mantra. At one point Tony shared a story. He said,

"If you are a good husband;
a good father;
a good business owner
or a good leader guess what?
You're gonna to achieve
mediocre results

If you an excellent father;
husband; or business owner you
may produce good results.

However if you choose to be
outstanding in all of those roles,
you may get excellent results.

Excellent is OK but you will
only achieve it if you aim
higher"

The word outstanding means literally to stand beyond to stand above. Finally I found somebody who was talking that language. So from that day on I chose to always live my life in and outstanding way, because for sure by leaving outstandingly I could have excellent results.

On the 30th of October 2017 I opened my first UK company and guess what was its name Outstanding Services Ltd.

If you want to be successful, find someone who has achieved the results you want and copy what they do and you'll achieve the same results.

Tony Robbins

One of the main pillars of Tony's teachings is about standards, and this resonated with everything my mum taught me in my life. Never settle for mediocrity but always raise my standards higher.

This has determined the quality of my life; my emotional standards; and my physical standards. This is what generates and creates massive results in my life.

On the last day of the event, even though I had back row tickets, I was given the opportunity to walk across the stage. So there I was, on stage where the big man had performed!

I said to myself, this is where I belong. I am going to do what it takes to be on stage with him in the future. Apparently, at that moment, the Universe heard what I was saying

The following year, Tony Robbins returned to London, and of course, I had to be there. However, as I had participated in a previous event, I now qualified to volunteer as crew this time. I jumped at the chance.

This was an event for 13,000 people and it really felt like a huge family. Everyone was positive and on fire.

At the briefing session I volunteered to be on the Meet and Greet team. There were ten groups each of 100 people, so 1000 people devoted to making the first moment on arrival for the participants, positive and energetic. I knew that this was the job for me!

Then one of the team captains said that she wanted to drop out and buy a ticket, at full price, so that she could participate instead. Tony Robbins assistant was there and said "What are we going to do? We need somebody" – just at the moment I was walking past. Life is about opportunities and he looked straight at me and said "Will you be the captain?" I didn't know what to say, but I recovered quickly enough to say "Yes!"

Opportunities are fleeting things. They are there in a moment and gone in the next. All you have is a milli-second to recognize them and react. Wait too long and they have vanished. For me this was the right moment and I was in the right place. All my leadership experience and skill just surfaced when they were needed and my team absolutely rose to the occasion. And I had been noticed!

The meeting of preparation with opportunity generates the offspring we call luck.

Tony Robbins

Later, one of Tony Robbins' assistants selected me to do another specific task based on my level of commitment and 'my leadership energy'. I was selected to be on Tony Robbin's personal fire lane. He is always the first one to walk on fire and then he guides his top clients, the platinum members to do the same.

I had the chance to watch the big man getting in state and walking on fire. Then my job was to hold him while he celebrates and then do the same thing with his clients. There was only one rule. Do not stop him, interrupt or speak to him whilst he is in his state. I was just there to serve. Of course, I did what I was told.

I found it very inspirational to work with Tony in this way and to watch how he focussed himself to get into his State. I watched him making his move and walk with such certainty on those hot coals. Once I had helped all the people in Tony's fire lane to do their walks, it was the time for all of us volunteers to have our turn.

Building on my experience of doing the fire walk on Day One, I knew how I would get even more out of this experience this time. This time I did the fire walk thirteen times!

Each walk, I focussed on one single target I wanted to achieve in life. One single thing I wanted to remove; one single thing I wanted to overcome. A fear I wanted to conquer.

This time, I made the conscious decision to seriously raise the bar. I decided that was going to take my career another level it was time for me to move on up. The time was right for me to make another big decision in my life in order to achieve more.

I truly believe that everything that we do and everyone that we meet is put in our path for a purpose. There are no accidents; we're all teachers - if we're willing to pay attention to the lessons we learn, trust our positive instincts and not be afraid to take risks or wait for some miracle to come knocking at our door.

Marla Gibbs

I am a firm believer that nothing happens by accident. Everything is for a reason and we are all part of the great plan of the Universe. That doesn't mean to say that challenging things won't happen, it does mean that they have been sent to teach us something. We just need to find out what it is!

With all the things that had happened to me, including my ex-girlfriend literally burning all my bridges around me and making sure I would really be alone, I began to find meaning. I realised that many of the people that had been around me were not my actual friends. They were just there for their own self-interests and what they could get from me. Sad but true. This realisation helped to put things in perspective. I needed another seminar to help to get my head straight.

Life is a gift, and it offers us the privilege, opportunity, and responsibility to give something back by becoming more.

Tony Robbins

Chapter Nine

JUST ONE HOUR

After my first UPW, I came across a training that interested me about property sales and development with Kevin Green. It was interesting but I quickly realised that I would need far more capital than I currently had to make it work. That started me thinking about other areas of sales that could produce a big return. That's how I came across trading stocks and shares.

It was here that I met a man who was to have a great influence on my life, Rich Waterman. Apart from being an expert in the Stock Exchange, he announced that he was also a Tony Robbins trainer. Now he had my attention. We met after the event and the first thing he said to me as "I like your energy and your strong presence!" For me that was a great compliment because at that time I didn't feel very empowered. I was still rebuilding myself.

After the event, I checked out his website and discovered that he only coached high-achieving individuals and that he was also very expensive! I didn't believe I was enough of a high-flier for him to be interested in me and even if I was, I could not afford him. Anyway, I sent him an email wondering if he would be my coach. Much to my surprise, he wrote back saying that he wanted to talk to me because he wanted to work with people like me. On that basis I felt he had chosen me.

But I was honest with him and told him I was currently working as a waiter, and didn't think I could afford him. He gave me a proposal, still for a lot of money, to work with him for an hour a month. This was to be the springboard I needed.

Out of that one hour, I started growing and expanding far faster than ever before. This is the difference that a good coach can do for you –

even for just one hour a month! At my work in the restaurant , I evolved from being a waiter to being a supervisor. Then from a supervisor in one their venues to being a manager for a number of them. I had the responsibility for cashing up and closing the venues at the end of the day. I had been given big responsibilities.

There is no doubt that when Rich Waterman agreed to work with me for just one hour a month, this was a major turning point.

One hour might seem like a very short amount of time, but the value you can get out of it depends on the thought you put into planning for it.

At that time, I was working ten to twelve hours a day. As I was living in London I add a further two hours for travel. So that is fourteen hours. I wasn't sleeping much more than, maybe five hours a night, so that took me to nineteen hours. The rest of the time I would be reading or listening to audio tapes.

Rich taught me that you could get so much done in an hour. My one-to-one time with him was precious. I would plan by making notes in my journal of the things I wanted to talk about. In fact, by the time I got to meet him, many of the points I had prepared, I had already solved or received a deep insight into the answer. The brain is good at taking a problem, work on it in its own time and then give you the answer.

All you needed to do was to ask it! Most of us overestimate what we can achieve in a day, but underestimate what we can achieve in a month.

We have all proved that we can do more than we believe we can. What about the day before you were going on holiday? How much did you achieve in the final hour before you left?

For me, an hour is valuable time. I have learned the fruit of patience. I have learned the value of solitude and of giving myself time to think and process problems without noise. Much though I love music and it is a major part of my life I am not one of those people who spend every moment wearing white earbuds and anaesthetizing my brain with noise just to shield me from the danger of thinking.

There is a time for music and there is a time for quiet.

For me, the hour a month I spend with my coach gives me alternative ways to look at things that you are too close to see. And we all have blind spots that we just can't or don't want to see. Whatever you do, find your hour and find your mentor. If it is not me, then find somebody else.

All the great successful people in the world have a mentor or a coach. Coaching is not to fix you, you are not broken. Coaching is for people who are successful and for people who are hungry to become even better They want to go even further and achieve great things. So, find yourself your coach, get your Hour of Power, and you will be surprised where will you where you will be in the next five years.

Tony Robbins once said that

if you want to conquer an island, you start by burning the boats.

So that's what I did. I wrote a letter of resignation to the owner of the bar I was working at. As soon as he received it, he called me right away and asked me to reconsider. He even offered to double my wages. But as doubling my wages only took me to £14 an hour, I knew I was worth much more than that. So I left.

Through my coach, I had built myself up ready for the next level. There was no going back. The big lesson that I learned was that, sometimes life will not happen the way you wanted it to simply because you are not ready. What use would being a millionaire have been if my money mindset was still focussed on pennies. Without the maturity to use money wisely, it would just have been wasted.

I learned that the Universe presents opportunities to you once you are ready, and not before. These days I fully appreciate money and I am capable of making for more mature decisions. When I was a waiter, I am still grateful for every plate I have put on a table and every tray I have carried. Each of them brought me to where I am today. To each customer who said to me "Wow!, thank you so much for your service. Why are you working here?" Thank you.

So now I was ready for my next big move. I had resigned my position in advance of getting a new one. I wrote to the organisers of Tony Robbin's event is the UK and asked them for a job. They invited me for an interview. It's now down to me!
I arrived looking like a business owner. I had my navy blue suit, and a light blue powder shirt. Always dress to impress! I had an interview with the director who asked me what role I would like. I said anything! Even cleaning toilets. I just want to work here. They said, OK, there is a role in sales. Great!

I discovered that sales were done on the phone, which suited me perfectly. Having run an outbound telesales company in Italy, I knew I could make this work. They offered me the job selling on commission which was perfect because I knew there was no limit to my earnings.

Our job was to sell tickets to the next Antony Robbins event. I looked around at the other sales people. All of them were going for the lowest price tickers. The low-hanging fruit. So I asked the director, what was the most expensive product?

He told me it was Business Mastery and the top price was $10,000 per ticket, but not everyone could sell it.

I have never been afraid of big numbers so I said, "I would like to give it a try" and he said Okay.

I decided to use a coaching approach on my sales calls. With a high ticket item, people tend to think twice before making a commitment. In my experience, it is a lot more than twice! I explained the benefits they would gain by attending and compared that with what would happen if they don't get enrolled. I was levering pain and pleasure. By doing that, I was able to take a client from point A, where they are at the time, two point B, where they want to be. The vehicle was this business mastery programme of Tony Robbins, which is a five day program. I realised that it's not easy to take a business owner away from their business and their family for five days so I developed a method, and using this method I personally sold over $600,000 sales for this event. More than anyone else.

After the event, I spoke to my coach and told him what I had achieved and asked him where should I be going from here? After you have achieved something extraordinary, there is a dangerous moment when you relax when you think that the job is done. I knew that I had to keep my energy and momentum going.

An engine is at its most efficient when it is warm. I felt I needed to search for what my next 'More' was going to be.

Rich said to me, "With what you have achieved for this event, maybe you should spread your wings further and become a direct representative for Tony Robbins and be responsible for developing an entire country. With my business partner at that time Totka Spasova, we took up that opportunity and signed a contract to be the sole representative for Tony Robbins in Bulgaria. It was a huge step up going from serving behind a bar to serving a nation.

The first time I spoke in Bulgaria I had an audience of 600. This included top business leaders and the former President of the country. My work there grew quickly and we ended up coaching the national Olympics team and helping young people realise that they could be far more than they could ever have dreamed.

The reward for work well done is the opportunity to do more.

Jonas Salk

Chapter Ten

TAKING TIME TO LEARN

By sharing my story with you, you can see that, despite the mistakes I have made along the journey, there are a number of qualities I have had to develop, which have made all the difference.

The first is Discipline.

When I started my first business I wasn't disciplined and I didn't have a plan, so it was never going to end well. I made plenty of other mistakes along the way like not asking for legal advice, and not having regular meetings with my accountant. I didn't understand or anticipate the market. So I was like a little kid trying to do business with his gigantic ego in front of everything he was trying to do.

Having a plan means you only need to focus of doing one thing at a time and getting it right before you move on to the next step.

It is the Discipline that helps you to persevere to do so. You can drive from London to Glasgow at night by only seeing the next 30 yards ahead of you in the headlights. One step at a time is all you need.

In addition, people who are disciplined are the ones who have more self-esteem. Self-esteem is not a gift or talent but something that you build up constantly and consistently day by day. Why?

Because, when you keep your word, you keep your word to the most important person on earth – to yourself. You are the one person you cannot fool. You are the one person that you need to be true to. Your self-esteem grows with you.

The long-term rewards of staying disciplined and for shrugging off those little lapses in determination, are huge. You build up strength of character and confidence in yourself and of what you now have the strength to achieve.

Discipline is the bridge between goals and accomplishment.

Jim Rohn

When I talk to my athletes, and work with them, I always tell them to keep working on the basics, the ABC principles. Doing the basics is part of discipline. Every day you should be working on the three things that you are most grateful for.

One of those things could be reading a book that inspires you or teaches you. Reading just 30 pages a day should be a discipline. Listening to positive news should be part of your discipline. Asking sorry when you have not lived up to your own standards. All of these should be a part of your daily discipline.

Having more discipline in your life has to be something that you want to embrace, and something that you want to always welcome in your life. In your household. If you teach kids to be disciplined from a young age, with all of their daily routines, rituals and behaviours, when they become adults, other disciplines will be much easier for them. You need to start young.

Finally, in this subject, whenever I did something wrong, my mom never punished me. She came from the British tradition of education, and would always teach me to understand where I had gone wrong so I could make better choices next time. For her Discipline did not mean punishment but encouragement to make the right choices.

I do like to analyze words and to break them into separate parts. As I thought about the word Discipline, I linked it with the word Disciple and the concept of voluntarily acting in a specific way in certain circumstances irrespective of how you might feel.

Make being disciplined, one of your major skills. Be disciplined with yourself and also be disciplined with the people who are around you. Be known for having the strength to make the right choices in everything you do.

The Curse of the Creative

I have always been at my most energized when I was being creative. For me, being creative means working with music, with writing, or with being on stage and speaking from the heart. It is also when working with coaching clients and helping them to reframe their circumstances or their lives. Being creative requires being very much in the moment and allowing the brain to make exciting new connections. Creativity is all-consuming. consuming.

Be brave enough to live life creatively. The creative place where no one else has ever been.

Alan Alda

The downside of this is when that those skills overflow into everyday life. It is one thing for the brain to jump from idea to idea, it is another when you are jumping from task to task and never completing them before moving on to something else. I know there have been times when I have been very guilty of this, and my team has urged me to slow down and finish what I had started. It has always been my enthusiasm that has driven me.

If you are not careful, you can leave a pile of unresolved problems behind you on the road, as you rush forward to the next exciting project. It is an easy trap to fall into! Have you been there yourself?

I believe that depression is a lack of expression. People who have no outlet for creative expression can become very internal, very anti-social and a danger to themselves. When you are depressed, you have no purpose or direction. For me, when I am creating, I am expressing my talent, expressing my gift. I am truly alive.

When I am creating a program, creating a blog or an essay, or just getting out one of my instruments and playing them, it is all a part of my creative journey. It's part of my creative expansion, it's part of my expression. And I love it

Playing music is a way of channeling my creativity. But it can be addictive. So getting lost in creativity may lead you to not being able to conclude, finish, complete, and remain grounded. Nobody wants to have the reputation of being brilliant but not finishing what they started.

It is also possible to be too creative. This can mean adding too much complexity, layers, or elements. I have learned that Complexity is the enemy of execution. The more complex something is, the more difficult it is to make. You could be put off from starting by the thought of how complex it is. Simplicity might be the answer

If you are to be successful as a creative, you will need to bring together the ability to both create and also complete. Every day when we open our computers, we open several different windows each with a different function. We work in those windows to complete our tasks. Those windows usually remain open on the screen all day. At the end of the day, you need to complete the task in each window before you can close down the machine. This is discipline.

No matter what people tell you, words and ideas can change the world.

Robin Williams

If you get distracted with random thoughts arriving when you are in the middle of something else, you need to find a way of parking them till you are ready to deal with them.

In the past, I used to use post-it notes or a small notebook. Once I had written down the idea, I could move on and not worry about forgetting it. .

One of my treasured possessions are the many journals I have filled with ideas over the years. There is something very satisfying about revisiting a handwritten journal and discovering nuggets of gold waiting there.

Now with technology, there are multiple ways of recording information, such as tablets and smartphones so we have no excuse. This technique can be helpful in other ways as well.

I had a client, Robert (not his real name) who had a lot going on in his mind. He was overwhelmed with everything going on in his company and also in his team. At his next coaching session I told him to get a notebook and to write down every single thought that entered his mind. Everytime that he was worried, afraid or angry, just write it down.

Doing this, he found it easier to focus on each individual task and he became less stressed and was able to make better decisions.

As a result of doing this he became better able to put things into context and to take better decisions. This is the power of offload. It really works.

Every single thought, every single fear, every single situation that you cannot manage, isolate it by writing it down.

The more details you add to it, the better. And when you put that down in black and white, you suddenly free your mind. Let your brain work on it offline. It will tell you when it has found a solution.

As you free your mind you also change your physiology. You need to have sufficient mental RAM to process everything in turn. Cluttered thoughts cause paralysis.

Developing the ability to offload, you able empty your brain of worries, fears and negative thoughts. You've created space. Now you have created space to listen to what the universe is trying to tell you. You already have all the answers to your fears and problems. You just need to give yourself space to work them out.

Habits

In order to become more disciplined, we've got to create new habits. So how do you create new habits to push away the old ones? How do you structure a new habit from scratch?

First of all, we need to understand and come to the deep realization as a human beings, we are already creatures of habit. We actually prefer to do things the same way - it means that we don't need to think. We always take the same route to the shops or to the school.

I bet that whenever you go to work or wherever you go and do something, you always go the same way. When you drop your kids to school, you drop them in the same place. We love habits!

Once we get to like a restaurant, we make it a habit of going to it regularly. We know what to expect.

Of course, not all habits are good. I believe that, if we are serious in changing a bad habit, the only solution is to replace it with a good one.

Habit is something that has been constantly repeatedly and reinforced. There's this saying in the self-development world that it takes 21 days is to create a new habit, simply by repetition.

I never could have done
what I have done without the
habits of punctuality, order,
and diligence, without the
determination to concentrate
myself on one subject at a time.

Charles Dickens

And once that repetition, has become part of you, in 90 days, that becomes a lifestyle. For example, have you ever tried not to drink coffee with sugar?

As an Italian, coffee used to be for me, a major element in my life. It was a habit. At one point I was drinking more than eight to ten espressos a day. Maybe a bit too much.

I was in the habit of adding sugar. Then for a change, I started having it without. That became my new habit. Now, I cannot drink it with sugar at all. And then I decided to get rid of coffee all together. The first time it was hard, because it was a new habit. But by reinforcing it and reinforcing well, I gave it up entirely.

Now I can tell you that as an Italian, not drinking coffee at all for three years, was a big achievement.

One word here that we need to remember is the word conditioning. I conditioned myself not to drink coffee.

An athlete does not become a champion overnight. A successful business owner doesn't become a success overnight. This is how it might appear to the world, but the world doesn't see the time you spent to make it happen.

We need to deliberately create positive and empowering habits to condition ourselves. Habit is not only just repetition, the other half is conditioning yourself.

When you want to create a new habit, you need to emotionally attach pain and pleasure. Most of the time, we are afraid of losing something. So if you want to create a new habit in your life, use the leverage and the power of pain and pleasure to condition yourself.

Pain may push you, but pleasures should pull you towards the success you are after and towards that achievement.

I once had a client client who wanted to stop smoking. "Moses, please help me to stop smoking" he pleaded. So I asked him, tell me about your family and your kids. "My kids are fine!" he said "but they hate me smoking."

Apparently they hated the smell and wouldn't cuddle or kiss him because of it.

I asked him, how would you feel if, because of the small of cigarettes, she didn't want you to walk up the aisle when she gets married? What if she didn't want you to be close to your grandchildren because of the cigarettes?

So what I was doing was linking pain to an emotion. I knew he had tried various therapies to quit smoking which had not worked for him. There was also no point in focussing on the money that cigarettes were costing him because he could well afford it. So I did two sessions with him linking pain and pleasure. I painted the picture of the pain of not being able to take the daughter to the wedding, not being able to meet his grandchildren, and being an influence on their lives. As a result, he decided that his daughter was more important than a cigarette.

Whatever you are trying to change, you need to condition yourself because you don't get successful just doing something once. Look at the gym. You don't make your muscles by going to the gym only once it's the consistency it's the habit that you create.

One of the fastest ways to create a habit is by modelling.

Giving up smoking is the easiest thing in the world. I know because I've done it thousands of times.

Mark Twain

Ask yourself, who is your role model? You should be looking out there for somebody who is achieving or doing what you want to achieve.

You can then look up to them for the inspiration to achieve what they are doing. When you model you are creating a new habit, which you then need to reinforce.

It is easier now, because social media can help you to identify potential coaches, mentors are role models, and to make it easy to follow them. Technology can help widen your search worldwide and to follow the people that interest you. Don't forget also, that you might be the role model that somebody else is looking for So be open.

We live in a society where everything now is based on appearance, everything is fame. Everything is based on the number of Likes and how many followers you have.

I believe that it's not all about how many fans and followers and people who know me. The only way to impress people is living life with authenticity, and not trying to copy something that others are doing that is not worthy.

Most of the time we try to impress people that we don't like or don't even know. We live in a society where we always want to prove or please and make people understand how successful we are. Just buying a particular brand of T-shirt or wearing or a pair of branded sneakers, that's not success.

Find role models that inspire you, and role models with values, not role models that are all just about appearances.

Ask yourself, what can I learn from them that can really impact my life? How can I then impact people around me and add value to thier lives?

People are also looking at you all the time and at the way you present yourself. You know that they are looking for people to follow. They're looking for people with qualities and values. So you need to be mindful about how you're projecting yourself - and also who you are following.

One of the elements that always snaps me back to reality is the question, "Who out there is looking at me?" not because I need to impress them, but because I know that somebody's looking at me trying to get inspiration. So the first thing is, I don't want to let down myself. And I don't want to let down other people. So this is an element of contribution.

If I can contribute to you, without anything in exchange, that's the highest way of contributing. There are people who are looking at you right now. And there are people who would like you to be their role model.

All the life experience you have accumulated over the years; all those times you have faced difficulties and overcame them; all those times when you were in an impossible situation, but managed to get through it, these are all great assets you have with which to help others.

You challenge is to be aware of those around you and to look for ways of sharing your gifts. If you are open, the Universe will bring those people to you who are in the most need. You need to do the rest!

Everyone in society should be a role model, not only for their own self-respect, but for respect from others.

Barry Bonds

Gratitude is the healthiest of all human emotions. The more you express gratitude for what you have, the more likely you will have even more to express gratitude for.

Zig Ziglar

Chapter Eleven

THE IMPORTANCE OF GRATITUDE

When I started looking at the title of this book, I chose 'More'. I knew that there would be some people who would think I was being selfish and wanting to just generate MORE in my life or for myself. This was not the case.

My focus was to discover those qualities, and values in my life which would enable me to share the gifts that I had been given. I wanted to help everyone I met or worked with, to get MORE in their lives. My legacy will be measured not by te size of my my house, my car or the size of television I have, but rather how well I have inspired others to get MORE in their lives.

I know from my own experience that the one thing that has attracted many good things in my life is having an Attitude of Gratitude.

When I look round at everything I have, the people that the universe has brought to me and the opportunities surrounding me, I cannot fail to be hugely grateful.

Gratitude is the highest form of consciousness. Through gratitude, we get access to our Creator and the Universe, whatever that means to you. This is not about religion, it is about the simple acknowledgement that there is something bigger out there than ourselves. Recognising the spiritual aspect to our lives adds a new and exciting dimension to everything.

No one who achieves success does so without acknowledging the help of others.
The wise and confident acknowledge this help with gratitude.

Alfred North Whitehead

Gratitude is the key to how you remove any type of selfishness. It is no longer just about you. It allows you to become a co-creator of circumstances along with your Creator. So, one of the first things for you to be able attract more in your life is to develop an attitude, where being grateful is a fundamental part of your life. Because you get in life, not what you want, but what you are. The more you're grateful, the more the universe, and the more your Creator will want to create more with you. And you become part of the co-creation.

When I am working with with my athletes, and with my clients, I task them every day with focussing on three things that deeply grateful for. This is a great habit to get in to! The moment you focus on those three things that you are grateful for, you expand, and you get into that new dimension.

When I do this myself, I realise that I am rich in so many ways. Being rich is nothing to do with money. But I am abundant. I feel healthy. The more you are aware of that, the more you vibrate in those frequencies, the more you attract into your world.

As with every aspect of improving ourselves, developing this attitude is something you need to work on every day. This is what I call conditioning. You need to condition yourself. It's not about reading one book and believing you have you have learned that lesson for life. Anything worthwhile needs to be worked on everyday.

The trouble with things that are easy to do, is that they are easy NOT to do. Unless we consciously turn things into a habit other things will get in the way. Distractions are everywhere!

When I am coaching professional athletes, they are training every single day. No matter how long they have been in their particular sport, I insist that they practice the basics every single day. The amateur practices till they get it right. The professional practices till thay cannot get it wrong! Practicing your attitude of gratitude is one of those fundamentals

Some people say to me that they don't have anything to be grateful for. That would be so sad if it were true. But is is not. They are simply allowing the negative things in their life to eclipse all of the many positives things that might be hidden from them at that moment.

At the very least, all of us can be grateful for our parents, or whoever raised us, and gave us the education that enabled us to read. This gave us the ability to learn and grow.

Be thankful that you live in a free country and have the ability to make choices for your future.

Take nothing for granted!
Everything is a gift.

Gratitude is the magnet that will attract more to you everyday. Take a moment to look around you in your circle of family and friends. I am sure you will not have to look far to find someone who is miserable or is always complaining. They don't smile. They don't laugh, they are stuck in a bubble of gloom of their own making. Their focus is on materialistic things, mainly those they don't have. Their only interest is in themselves and dragging those around them down to their level.

I have heard it said that everyone lights up a room. Some when they arrive, others when they leave! Which are you?

Compare those to who you like to be around. The people who smile when they see you. Those who are genuinely interested in you and what is happening in your life. They are easy to talk to. They laugh often and are always appreciative, and supportive. They don't complain or criticise and always put others needs before their own. So which would you like to spend more time with?

Your attitude and the way you think, is expressed in the words you use to the people around you. Your ready smile, your willingness to listen and to look for ways of helping. The spark inside you can light up a room or a country. It is how you choose to use it.

If you have not done this before, I recommend getting an Gratitude Journal and making an entry in it everyday. Write down things you are proud of, good things that happened and the people who made your day special.

On those days when you are challenged or when something bad happens, it can be very encouraging to have some positives to help put things into perspective. Tony Buzan, the inventor of Mind Mapping, was known for reacting to challenging events by saying "How fascinating!" He would never react with a negative. It is your fundamental attitude to every situation that you will be known for. And everything is connected! Developing your attitude is just like developing a muscle, you have to work on it every day.

The most important thing to remember is that

Attitude is a choice.

In every situation, before reacting to it, there is a millisecond of decision making time in which you can choose how you are going to react. When I discovered this it changed my life. Like it or not, we are all pre-programmed on how to react in any given situation.

When something goes wrong we get annoyed. It is only natural. However, it is a choice of how we express that negative emotion. We can react or we can choose not to react. Whichever we choose will have a consequence. It will influence those around us one way or another.

In London's West End there are plays and musicals taking place every night. No matter which day you go to see a show, you know you can rely on a perfect performance from each of the cast members. They will be energetic, funny, positive and totally professional at every performance. Does that mean for the rest of the day, they exhibit those same qualities? Certainly not! They are human beings, not robots! However, a skill that they have developed is the art of total focus and living in the moment. It is called Theatrical Flair. It is the ability to assume a role for a particular purpose. It is a choice and a valuable skill whether you are on stage as a performer, or assuming the role of a manager in front of your employees.

I believe our greatest source of inspiration is to observe the actions and the words of others.

The universe has a wonderful way of bringing people into our lives to help teach us life's great lessons. Some people are with us for a reason and some for a season. One thing is for certain, there is no such thing as coincidence. We are all exactly where we are meant to be at every moment and are all a part of a great divine plan.

We need three types people around us. Firstly, those we need to lead. So these are people who look up to us and can benefit from what what we have learned on our journey so far. They will follow us on social media, attend our courses and buy our books. We have a responsibility to them to give them our best help and guidance.

Then there are a group of people that we can laugh with and grow with. These are our peer group, people who are on the same journey with us, so we can be open, we can relax, we can be friendly. There is mutual respect and mutual support. We acknowledge that we are all work in progress and so welcome the advice offered to us.

And finally, there is the group of people we look up to. These are the people who inspire us, who we follow, and whose books we read. These are the people we respect and appreciate.

We need all three types of people around us for us to fulfil our purpose.

To help you with this chapter, get a copy of the Moses Nalocca Gratitude Journal. Go to www.mosesnalocca.com/book/journal

Chapter Twelve

WORDS OR ACTIONS?

One of the biggest misconceptions in the self-development world is that many people believe that knowledge is power. If that were the case, then every professor would be driving a Porsche instead of a bicycle! So what is missing?

Knowledge, on its own, is potential power but only if you bring it from the theoretical world, into to the practical and tangible. The fastest way to do this is to take action. Action is the key.

Look at Wikipedia. It is full of knowledge and full of facts. You can find an answer to almost any question. But it won't tell you how to use that knowledge. Applied Knowledge is when somebody has solved a problem or developed a process and shares that experience in such a way that others can follow that process and achieve a result. The knowledge on its own is own no use without action.

You are the one that can make something real and tangible. In 1956, Earl Nightingale wrote "The Strangest Secret" in an attempt to teach people the power of the mind, the power of thought. He said,

"You become what you think about all day long."

Nightingale's inspiration came from Napoleon Hill's book, **"Think and Grow Rich,"** published in 1937. However, is that really true?

In 2006, the author Rhonda Byrne launched the DVD and subsequently the book called **'The Secret',** all about the Law of Attraction which further develops the concept of thoughts drawing things towards us. Certainly, thoughts can indeed manifest opportunities, but to turn them into something tangible, action needs to happen. The results will always be down to what we do. Action always is the key.

FOCUS

Another quality which has helped me achieve some truly spectacular results is to develop the ability to focus. Initially I was confused about this word. Everyone was telling me 'Focus, Focus!' and I wasn't sure what they wanted of me.

Then I heard the phrase that help make it make sence

"Follow One Course Until Success".

I got it and it was a major turning point in my life.

First of all, I realised that I was doing just too many things at the one time. I was spreading my wings everywhere. I was doing everything. I was going everywhere. I was listening to everybody. My life was too full and unstructured.

I was so anxious to feed my mind with the right things that I was falling into the trap of travelling anywhere to visit a training event in the hope that I would pick up that one nugget of gold that would make all the difference. I was not focussed on using my precious time to best advantage.

When I focused, working only with my coach and following only one programme, that's the moment where I had more expansion and more growth. So when I was thinking that focus would limit me, instead, focus expanded me.

Looking back at my childhood, I remember that time when we, as a family, found ourselves with a huge debts and we had lost everything. We had to sell our house just to pay some of them, but there were many more. I became focussed on finding ways to pay them off and in that moment, I was focusing only on my debts. As I now know only too well, you get what you focus on. I realised that I was focusing all my attention on the lack of money, the debts and the problems. Guess what? Problems were increasing and debts were increasing. As Tony Robbins says,

'Where focus goes, energy flows.'

I heard that first at the T Harv Eker training I attended in Ireland but I only really understood it when I went to the Tony Robbins live event six months later. Only then did I understand that it was my focus that was wrong.

So, when I started focusing on how to add value, even in the pub where I was working, everything changed. I used focus to plan for my my holiday, something that I had not enjoyed for a very long time. I started to write down that things I wanted to do and to use my new found power of focus to achieve them.

I started to become far more aware of where I was putting my attention. I would catch myself out by checking what I was thinking about and asking myself, where was I putting my attention. So by understanding where I was putting my attention, I started shifting from scarcity, to abundance.

So I focused on my job in the pub, where I was working as a waiter and before long I was promoted to manager. In very little time, I ended up supervising with five venues in central London. I was successful, but I knew it wasn't where I wanted to be. I still wanted MORE.

> # Focus on the journey, not the destination. Joy is found not in finishing an activity but in doing it.
>
> ## Greg Anderson

Then the opportunity arrived for me to work in the Tony Robbins office. This was taking me closer to where I wanted to be. There was an event coming up and tickets needed to be sold. I could see this as an opportunity to prove myself, so asked to sell the most expensive tickets to the event, where everyone else was looking to sell the cheapest.

I applied by ability to focus and became the top salesperson generating over £600,000 in sales in just six weeks. An amazing achievement which gave me great confidence in my abilities. I now knew I was in the right place and was determined to make the most of it.

Seeing the wood from the trees

I have come to realise that focussing on my personal development, there are some things that I am too close to see properly. In the same way that doctors cannot heal themselves, none of us can step back far enough to see our own 'big picture'. So I looked for a coach to work with and found Rich Waterman (richwaterman.com). He only takes on a very few personal clients so I was very fortunate that he agreed to work with me.

At this point I was employed and doing well. The bills were being paid and I was comfortable. However, when you are hungry for MORE, being comfortable is not the greatest motivator for taking action. My coach arrived when I needed him the most.

I had always thought that I was a determined person but that was before I started to have nagging questions in my head. How badly do I really want this? Why should the universe give me this? Do I really deserve this? Do I really need this success?

Taking my mind back to the time when my family were deeply in debt, I had the mindset of 'do or die' which was not far from the truth and which drove my determination then. But this was now. My saying 'Do or die' seemed out of place It was no longer empowering me. Rich had the answer. Reframe it to 'Do it and thrive'!

Determination

So now my concept of determination morphed from Do or Die, into 'Do it and thrive'. I left what I would call my own power, my own human ability, which is limited. Because I have limited hours, limited resources, the moment has shifted from Do or Die to Do it and thrive, things have changed completely. Why? Because now it is, do it and I thrive. And now I've changed vibration of change frequency. Now my determination is the element that allows me to tap into the supernatural.

There are moments where I can't make it by myself, I need to tap into another dimension. I need to get into another level. I need to get into something else. So now determination becomes something to look for.

Determination does not only go with your own power, with your own ability, with your own personal capacity and ability. This is a supernatural element, call it Providence, call it grace, call it divine support, because now it's no longer me.

I am determined and I'm showing to the universe what I want. When I was younger, determination was related to what I want for me, me, me, me, me. Now determination has shifted in another way. Now I am determined to make a difference. So I can be a difference for others.
So this was my major shift.

I was not going beyond myself so why should the universe help me to achieve that goal?

Now, my determination was not aimed at myself but at how it could impact on others, It's not about me, it goes beyond me. And when it goes beyond me now I have grace, divine support and the universe supporting me.

I now truly understoob the words of Zig Ziglar,

"The only way you can get
what you want,
is to help enough
other people to
get what they want"

Genius!

Chapter Thirteen

STRONG FOUNDATIONS

Looking back. it is amazing to see how many of the qualities I now have, originate from my mother and the way she brought us all up. I thank her for ensuring that there was a strong spiritual dimention in our lives.

Not everybody has that foundation. And so many people drift off course because they don't have that strong anchor to keep them grounded. My spiritual upbringing has helped me to build on on those strong foundations and brought me to where I am today. I am really, really grateful for that.

Today, the world considers spiritual people as weak or who are cowards in life. Because they are cowards, they reason, they need to rely on an another entity. A strange way of thinking.

I believe spirituality to be something so intimate and personal. I believe spirituality is more a relationship. A relationship with the God inside of you.

And you don't need to give a name to that God because he is a part of you

Actually, I'm not religious. I'm spiritual. And I believe there's something great in each one of us. And it's our duty. It's our responsibility to tap into that greatness. And that is Your Divine connection.

I was raised up in a Christian family and I'm a Christian. I believe that each one of us has got this divine connection, this divine power within us because we are all in the divine image. So when people see you, they need to see a reflection of who truly you are.

Many people say "Oh, I can't see God, God does not exist. What are you talking about?" Well, we are all part of his wonderful creation. So you want to see God? Look inside yourself. You want to see God? Be the one to take action. You want to see God's kindness? Be the kindness. Because each one of us is a Divine Being and a spiritual being. It doesn't matter which denomination or which label we have put on ourselves. We created all of these labels. Not God.

There is both good and bad inside each of us but if all of us get back to our true relationship, our true connection, we will see that divine light in each one of us. So yes, spirituality, has been a strong element, in my life. It has been a foundation and helps me to do what I'm doing. Without it I would not love people the way I love them, I will not be as patient. Being spiritual has helped be to get thorough all the tears and hard moments on my journey. It can do the same for you.

Life can be kind of of ironic. In order to prepare and equip me to speak to you, to relate and connect with you, the Universe made sure I experienced and learned from all of the challenges that you have had. Without that, how can I possibly relate and understand you? I went through loss, emotionally, spiritually, physically, relationships issues in a family. That's how I can relate to you. I went through sickness. I went through pain. But it was that belief, that helped me to understand and learn from it.

The universe has a law for each one of us. There is abundance everywhere in nature. If you don't believe in God, and don't believe in divine intelligence, look at nature!

Who could have created those beautiful landscapes? Look at the trees. The trees are always expanding, always flourishing all the time. Look at the miracle of life. There's something which goes beyond ourselves. And we are all interconnected.

If you see the divinity in you then I need to respect that divinity in you. If not, I'm not acknowledging my divinity. So spiritually, it is more of our deep relationship with ourselves.

For many years, I didn't understand this. For many years I could not stand looking at the myself in the mirror. I didn't like the Moses I was seeing. There was a moment in my life where I could not even stand, my own presence, my body, my looks, and what I was saying.

This was one of the most painful moments in my life because I was not spiritually connected. The moment when I accepted myself exactly as I am, when I acknowledged and accepted the greatness that was residing in me, that's the moment when I tapped into my true spirituality, and that's the moment when I tapped into my greatness. That's the moment when life started using me.

So now, look at yourself in the mirror. Who do you see? Do you like them? What relationship have you got with self? What relationship have you got with your Creator? Whatever name you put on it is a relationship. It is in addition to the relationship you have with yourself. And it's a very personal relationship. And it's the reason why gratitude is such a fundamental part of our lives.

I never realised why gratitude was so important. When I truly understood this I really understood what it means to be searching for MORE but I was looking in the wrong place.

We live in a society where we are never satisfied with what we have. We are fixated on finding more money. We all need the latest gadgets. How many phones do we actually need? We want to own an exotic car like a Ferrari. We want to be able travel wherever we want to go and yes, we want more and more money to fund our lifestyle. Really? Are we that shallow?

On paper, we're living in one of the best eras in human history. There is abundance everywhere. Shops are crammed with everything we could possibly want. But does that make us happy or better people? No of course not! No matter how much is available, it could never be enough. In our materialistic world, we have an insatiable appetite for MORE.

More pairs of shoes, more bags, more watches, more cars, or a better car. Having the latest BMW is not enough when someone else has the latest Lamborghini. So you have to upgrade. Then you see someone with a helicopter, and you have to have one of those! What about a private jet? Or a private island?

This was the moment when I realised that I actually didn't need anything. Anything. I realised that I had absolutely everything I needed. That's the moment when I understood to power of gratitude. I am ashamed that it took me so long to learn this deep secret.

Do you seriously want more? Be grateful for what you've got. Being grateful for who you are.

Start every day by waking up and being grateful for who you are, who you are with and what you have around you.

I do this with my clients and make them write down every single day three things that they are deeply grateful for, as they wake up in the morning.

I invite you also to do this exercise. You will quickly realise how rich you are, how blessed and how wealthy you are. You do not need billions to be rich

Gratitude is the currency that allows us all to access to that divine power that spoke earlier. Because when you are grateful, guess what? Life wants to give us more anyway.

One day, I was out by the seaside with my nephew. He looked up to me and said "Uncle Moses, can I have an ice cream." Sure, I said let's get one. So we did. I bought him a cone with one scoop of vanilla ice cream on top. I told him don't jump and run but kids will always be kids and he ran and jumped. Not surprisingly, the scoop fell off. I saw the sadness in his eyes.

I said to him, "Don't worry, let's get another one." So on our way back he spots another kid with an ice cream but this one is larger and has three scoops, one on top of the other. "Uncle Moses," he says "Can I have one just like that?" Now, as a loving uncle, I'd like to give it to him.

The three scoops, but as a responsible individual, I don't need to him to fail again. So I gave him one scoop. I said "When you can manage this one scoop without dropping it then next time, I can give you more." When it comes to gratitude. The more you're grateful for what you've got, the more you will get more.

Be grateful for what you've got, be grateful for who you are, be grateful for your business, be grateful for your clients.

Some years ago I started business which later failed. I had been doing well and had great clients but I took my eye off the ball. I had not planned for 40% business taxes and had spent that money on items for the business.

I was so engrossed in what I was doing that I forget to be grateful to the universe for what it was giving me. And guess what? The Universe says "Let's not give that to Moses. He's not grateful. He's not appreciating it. So why should I give it to him? Why should I give him more?"

We are stewards of what has been given to us. We are stewards of our kids. We are stewards of our partners. And if we don't, if we're not grateful, and we don't exercise gratitude, the universe will say "What's the use of me giving you this amazing partner, if you're not taking care of them?" If you take a gift for granted, what the universe can give, it can also take away.

Now, every client, I teach gratitude, because it's the best medicine for any problem. It's the best cure for any difficulties and situations. And it's the fastest way for us to change perspective. When we find something to be grateful for - and it doesn't have to be the huge things - just to be the small things, recognise they are a gift.

When men first went to the moon, when they came back, they fell in depression. Because what else is there after that? Nothing they could ever experience in the future could ever compare.
I work with athletes to take them down the path to being the best in the world. A gold Olympic medal is the pinnacle of every athletes career. It is vital that they don't take it for granted and remain grateful for that moment.

So one of the secrets I share with my clients is gratitude. And let me ask you, what are you grateful for? Find three things that you are deeply grateful for, and you realise how blessed you are, how rich you are, and how your life is amazing. And how your life is way better than what you thought it could be. What are you grateful for? Who are you grateful for? Think about this every day.

The greatness of a man is not in how much wealth he acquires, but in his integrity and his ability to affect those around him positively.

Bob Marley

Chapter Fourteen

INTEGRITY

Integrity has been one of my most important values in life. When I was a young kid, I always wanted to have a career in Law. I could see myself as a young Perry Mason – the American TV detective - defending the weak and the poor against injustice. When somebody had been accused of a crime and their story and was not believed, he would get to the truth and stop an injustice happening. He was the one that inspired me to do the same. To this day, I can't stand injustice of any sort, not even watching it is the movies. It makes me angry and want to do something about it.

So when it comes to integrity, to explain what it means to me I would like to break the word down in an orthodox way. I see it as two parts 'In' and 'Gratitude'. I know that any etymologist would tell me that this was not correct, but bear with me!

When you are 'into gratitude', and you are living a life of gratitude, you are living in the present and you're not worried of what's going to happen later on. When you are in this mind set, there is no way that you would take advantage of another human being. So for me 'integrity' means living a live 'in-gratitude'

I was watching an old movie recently with Mel Gibson called Apocalypto. It was an epic historical adventure set in Mexico following the doomed Maya civilisation. The Maya, believed that sacrificing human beings would be pleasing to pleasing to their gods. This philosophy wiped them out as a people. It was a lesson as to what can go wrong with an entire people when they have the opposite values to integrity and gratitude.

We have seen this over the centuries and around the world as brutality takes over common sense and common decency. When you are in gratitude, you cannot take advantage of another human being, when you are in gratitude, you cannot lie, deceive, steal, and worse, kill another person.

When you are living in integrity you cannot be in a state of fear. When you are in gratitude, you can be in a state of anxiety, when you are in gratitude, you can't be in a state of not feeling good enough, so you would never need to take advantage of somebody else.

You see, there are two ways to be the best. To be the greatest builder, you either build higher skyscrapers, or you demolish the other ones so they cannot compete with yours. Two very different mindsets.

To give real service you must add something which cannot be bought or measured with money, and that is sincerity and integrity.

Douglas Adams

Another way of looking at integrity is to do with how well you keep your word and keep your promises. This is where even your self-esteem either increases or diminishes as a result of what you do. This not just about the big things, but the small ones as well. It is about your promise to be at a certain place at a certain time. Unless you arrive when you promised, you have not kept your promises.

Being on time might seem a small thing, but it is not. You eighter planned to be on time, or you planned not to be. If you planned to be on time, you would have planned to be there fifteen minutes early in come you were delayed. That way you go into the meeting refreshed and in the moment. If you only plan to arrive on time, then you will be stressed and out of breath. This disrespects the person you are meeting. It is all about intention and planning.

When you arrive late, not only have you let the other person down, but you have let yourself down. No matter what disruptions or delays there are, you can always plan a strategy to overcome them. You wouldn't be late to meet the King would you? It is not the person, but the principle.

It is the same with making New Year's resolutions. My advice is not to make them lightly. If you are going to make one, do so wholeheartedly, and mean it. Don't promise yourself something if you don't really mean it, because if you do, and them break it, you have let yourself down and damaged your self-belief and self-esteem. Why would you want to do that?

If you promise to stop smoking or promise to go to the gym every day, and then drop out after a few days or a few weeks, you are damaging yourself. Far better not to make a resolution than to do so and not keep it. You diminish yourself and this is not integrity.

So rather than making a resolution, make a choice. A choice is far more powerful and easer to do because it is a binary decision. It is a yes or a no. A resolution is just an intention. You can choose to be on time. You can choose to keep your word. You can choose to do something or not to do something. You are in charge. You are making a commitment with yourself. If you don't then keep that commitment you are on a slippery slope because you cannot believe a word that you say – never mind everybody else.

Make the choice to always keep your word, to be the sort of person that can be relied on, and then people will know what you stand for. They will also know what you will accept and tolerate. They will know that, because you have high expectations of yourself, you will have those same expectations of others. They will know that you expect them to be on time and to do what they promised to do. You will be the cause the change in others that you have made to yourself. They will not lie to you because you do not lie to yourself. They will not disrespect you because you never disrespect yourself. You can cause a powerful change in the people around you by always being in Integrity yourself.

When I am coaching or mentoring I am often asked "How can I increase my self-esteem?"

Well, self-esteem comes first of all, from discipline. Are you keeping in integrity with yourself? When you say you're going do something? Are you doing it for somebody else? Are you doing it for yourself? Are you in a pleasing mode towards others or not to yourself and neglecting yourself?

Earlier on in the book you will have read that when I was growing up I was devastated with people not accepting me. I wanted everybody to love me. I wanted to be always the nice guy. But that wasn't helping me be with integrity with myself.

I have to admit that, at that time I wasn't living in my integrity. I wasn't living in my gratitude, because I wanted to please others. Thank God now I'm free from the being affected by the judgement and opinions of others. From the opinion of others, I do not allow anybody's opinion to become my own reality. Because I'm now in integrity with myself.

I used to hate to be with myself. So I would always be getting busy. Busy with people busy with events busy working, so I could just get tired and just go to bed straight away. That's not living your life with integrity, in gratitude. Are you grateful for the person you see on the mirror? Are you grateful for the words you speak to yourself? How do you feel when you look at yourself in the mirror? Do you hate the person you see? Or you love the person you see?

I remember the lyrics from the Michael Jackson hit, "The Man in the Mirror"

I'm staring at the Man In The Mirror
I'm asking him to change his ways
And no message could have
been any clearer
if you wanna make the world
a better place.
Take a look at yourself, and
Then make a change"

So let me ask you – "Who do you see then you look in the mirror?"

What are you going to do about him or her?

Well, when you live your life with integrity, you just end up falling in love more and more with that person you see, and you love and you cherish and you desire to have more and more moments by yourself. Right now, if you asked me, what is your best time, your best moment? I would say my best moment is early morning, when I'm alone with myself.

I wake up, do my rituals, go to the gym, and then start my day in before the rest of the world wakes up. It is golden time!

I love my lonely moments. I used to hate them. But now I love them. Because those are the moments where I am with myself. I am myself. And there's some moments when in the weekends, I tell my team, I need at least half a day or a full day where I don't want to see or meet or talk to anybody. So I'm happy with myself, what do doesn't matter. I could be laying down, I could be reading, I could be doing anything.

But I love those moments. Those are my private moments. And that's when you are also in integrity with yourself. You're also into gratitude with all the universe and everything that surrounds you know,

In solitude the mind gains strength and learns to lean upon itself.

Laurence Sterne

Chapter Fifteen

What are you afraid of?

Fear is something that has affected us all at some point or another. Whether as a child being frightened by a loud noise or an over friendly pet; whether at school and being bullied or whether later in life when bigger things get out of proportion and scare us. We all know what fear feels like.

George Busey is credited for the mnemonic for the word F.E.A.R. "False Evidence Appearing Real" - It's the darkroom where Satan develops his negatives."

Whatever has frightened us in the past, unless we can find a way of neutralising it in our minds, it can have the potential to haunt us in the future.

Having been brought up as a Christian, I tend to allow my faith to override my fear. Faith tells us that we are exactly where we are meant to be and to trust in God to see us through. So I grew up telling myself I was not afraid, time and time again where really I was scared out of my wits. Sometimes it worked. Mostly it didn't. Maybe this was really a lack of faith.

In the course of career, I have worked with literally thousands of people, and I have learned a lot from them. They have taught me that, at the end of the day, fear is something that is part of our nature. And instead of fighting it, and trying to destroy it, we should learn to dance with it.

Let me explain myself. When a child is born they have only two fears, a fear of starving and the fear of falling down. There is nothing else they fear. Then one day an uncle will pick him up and raise him high over his head. The child has no experience of this before as is terrorised by being so high. Next time it happens they know what to expect and start to see the pleasure in it. So we overcome some fears through our experiences through our lives. Other fears we learn from our journey.

Having fears does not make us a weak person but to be fully in our strength we have to acknowledge them, understand them, and face them head on. It is only then that we fully understand the true meaning of "False Evidence Appearing Real" and we realise that we have been conned and that things were not as we had imagined them to be.

It would be reckless it, when you were driving a car, not to have a healthy fear of a cyclist pulling our in front of you and causing you to swerve into another car. This healthy fear causes up to be more alert and to drive proactively. You would be foolish when climbing a mountain, not have a healthy fear of falling, and to take precautions to stop that happening. Having healthy fears are a good thing if they keep us safe. It is the irrational fears that we need to address.

If you were to listen to the news, it is full of many things to be afraid of. In fact the news can easily terrify some people. It takes wisdom to realise that there is nothing to be gained by worrying about things that we cannot do anything about. It is a fact that the vast majority of things that could happen, never will and worrying about them is fruitless.

It makes no sense to worry about things you have no control over because there's nothing you can do about them, and why worry about things you do control? The activity of worrying keeps you immobilized.

Wayne Dyer

There will always be genuine fears that do have the potential of compromising your safety, or of being catastrophic in other ways, were they to happen. These you cannot ignore and you need to address. What I do is to step back, pause and ask myself this question. Suppose this did take place, what is the worse that could happen? Will you die? Will your family abandon you? Will you be destitute? What is the absolute worse thing that could happen? When you look at it, It might not be as bad as you fear. You need to isolate it, put in into context and decide on the most appropriate course of action. The wrong thing to do is to panic!

In some cultures, the word Death means separation. To die is to be separated; separated from this physical reality; separated from the people that you love; and separated from yourself.

So, if Death is the worst case scenario, in whatever form, then anything else we can deal with, no matter how unpleasant or challenging. You can deal with any challenge if you can isolate it to precisely what it is – or isn't. Again, False Evidence Appearing Real.

Almost always our biggest problems are only in our heads and in our imagination. They are not actually reality. It is our interpretation of circumstance and our belief of what people might do or say that creates a negative picture which then goes on to fill our minds. We need to learn to dance with our fears and embrace them.

When my dad left us with all that huge debt, I had a lot of things to take care of for my family. Yes, I was afraid. I was afraid of losing everything. In fact, we lost everything. But I didn't lose my mom; I didn't lose my brother; I didn't lose the trust that people had in me: I didn't lose the owner of my name; I didn't lose the integrity of who I was; I didn't lose the love for others, and the love for our community and my church. What I gained was an opportunity to build my character. If I can get through this, I can get through anything. Fear can no longer have any grip on me

I am fearless. Nothing can hold me back ever again.

Spending time with fear is time lost forever

Another thing is that fear can create pain. Pain is an important feeling because it causes you to take action and makes you move. If you are in pain, there is something seriously wrong with your body that needs you to take action to put right.

Whether you have picked up a hot pan from the stove which could burn you or whether you are cut by a sharp object, pain is the body telling you to act – right away.

Fear can cause stress and stress can cause pain. This applies to your health, your finances, your relationships, indeed every aspect of your life. Pain means you need to act right away.

Take action, shift, pivot, reverse a situation. And if you don't pay attention to that pain, guess what happens? You end up suffering. But once to do take the right action, then our strength returns as does our integrity, our ability to be back in control and the possibility of turning things around. Now we go and deal with that pain and we deal with that fear and we dance with it. Fear will never go away from you, but if you recognise it quickly, it will never control you.

Fearless means trusting your instincts and clarity of thought. Once you have made up your mind, don't be scared of what if.

Ravi Shastri

Chapter Sixteen

BEING AT THE TOP
OF YOUR GAME

A number of my client are elite athletes and are striving for peak performance. This is never achieved overnight and it can take years to hone their stills so that they can compete with the top athletes in the world. Being a world class athlete is a long game. You need to prepare for something that is only going to take 10 to 20 seconds, or three minutes at the most, and it's over. You need to be at your absolute best for that tiny window of time.

In competitive sport, it is easy to think that all of the competitors are focused on beating each other. This is not the case. I tell my athletes, your battle, your competition is not against anybody else and certainly not against your opponent. Your biggest battle is with yourself.

Because the version of yourself that you know so far is a version which has gone through disappointments, through suffering, through pain, through loss. And that's the person you know.

So what I do with my athletes, we create a new version of themselves. Not based on the future, because this becomes quite dangerous, because you live your life always in the future and not in the present. We create a new version of yourself, which is present there in that moment.

So basically, what I do with my athletes is that we trade expectation for appreciation. What does that mean?

If you live your life all is an expectation. You expect your parents to do this, you expect your husband to do this, you expect your wife to behave like that, you expect your kids to behave with sound mind. But what if we trade that expectation for appreciation, and we start learning to reduce is the expectation and increase the appreciation.

For example, there's one of my athletes had a private invitation to appear at an exclusive sports event. And he was panicking. "Should I take part? Should I perform?" He asked.

I reminded his that they invited him so he has nothing to prove. Reduce the expectation to show off and prove who you are. But increase the appreciation. Be grateful to have been invited Be grateful that they chose you. And the moment you reduce expectation and increase your appreciation, you will start performing in your best way.

So, as you are reading this, ask yourself what are you expecting from yourself? Because if you live your life with all as an expectation. You end up facing disappointment. Disappointment is an expectation not met.

But when you trade, your expectations for appreciation, now you're getting a new dimension, the dimension of possibilities, the dimension of grace. All my athletes have a lot going on in their lives and all of them have a very active internal dialogue. For them, the secret is to be able to turn off that noise in their mind and tell it to be quiet.

Switching off that internal dialogue is an essential first step to clearing your mind so you can be truly present in the moment. For an elite athlete, that moment can be just seconds.

Do athletes get afraid? Of course they do! The expectation on them are enormous. It is not just the expectations of family and friends but also of their backers, sponsors, their coach and their team plus the expectations of the country they represent. If they allow all of that noise to fill their minds they would freeze with fear. The mind can be very quick to tell us what we can't do, and the times we had failed in the past.

Dwelling on these thoughts can flood our brains with negatives and doubts. Without disciplining our minds to overcome its natural tendency to sink down into negatives, we can never raise our game to its full potential. Our greatest competitor will always be ourselves.

So focus on what you are good at doing. Focus on all the multitude of things that you are truly grateful for. You need to keep reinforcing these thoughts time and time again so that they become your default mode of thinking

When you get into gratitude, your brain is awake, and your heart is leading you. And your heart will never lie to you. Your heart knows exactly what you need. Your heart knows exactly where you have to go.

But sometimes you need to shut down the noise in your brain and allow the heart, which is gentle, to lead you

You have more potential inside you than you could ever imagine.

Don't get in your own way to achieve the greatness that awaits you.

Moses

Resources

Let me invite you to join the,

MORE:
Official Moses Nalocca Community

https://www.facebook.com/mosesnalocca

https://www.instagram.com/mosesnalocca/

https://twitter.com/mjnalocca?lang=en

https://www.linkedin.com/in/mosesjnalocca/

https://www.youtube.com/channel/
UC8uomzdjPu2Bai_e4M0kMfw